GW00632684

RAMBLERS' WAYS

Edited by David Sharp

Ramblers'
Ways

DAVID & CHARLES
Newton Abbot   London   North Pomfret (Vt)

Drawings by Mark Richards

British Library Cataloguing in Publication Data

Ramblers' ways.
    1. Great Britain—Description and travel—
    Guide-books
    2. Trails—Great Britain
    I. Sharp, David
    914. 1'04'857   DA632
    ISBN 0-7153-7972-0

Library of Congress Catalog Card Number 79-56062

Edited © David Sharp 1980

Typeset by ABM Typographics Ltd., Hull
and printed in Great Britain by
Biddles Limited, Guildford, Surrey, for
David & Charles (Publishers) Limited
Brunel House   Newton Abbot   Devon

Published in the United States of America
by David & Charles Inc
North Pomfret   Vermont 05053   USA

Contents

Contributors

Colin Speakman was formerly Secretary of Ramblers' Association West Riding Area, and now a Principal Assistant with the Yorkshire Dales National Park. He is author of several books on walking in the Dales and on related subjects.

Fred Matthews is Secretary of RA West Essex Group, one of the Association's Footpath Secretaries for the county, and author of many path guides that have made West Essex popular with walkers. The Three Forests way was his own concept.

Brett Collier is Secretary of RA Lincolnshire and South Humberside Area, and Chairman of the Association's Lincoln Group. As a former college lecturer, he has run many rambling courses over the Lincolnshire Wolds and along the Viking Way.

Alison Kemp was Chairman of Oxfordshire Branch of the Council for the Protection of Rural England for four years, and is now a National Vice-Chairman. From its original conception, she has been a leading enthusiast behind the Oxfordshire Way and author of its guidebook.

Joe Turner is Secretary of RA Devon Area's Two Moors Way Subcommittee. He has been closely involved in surveying and maintaining the Way since the early seventies.

John Trevelyan is Deputy Secretary of the Ramblers' Association, and formerly their Footpath Secretary for Cumbria. In this capacity, with help from colleagues, he devised the Cumbria Way.

Jean Jefcoate is RA Footpath Secretary for Buckinghamshire, and Secretary of the Association's West London Group. With her team of helpers she has worked for years to protect the paths of the Vale of Aylesbury.

Geoffrey Berry is now Consultant Secretary of the Friends of the Lake District. As an outstanding photographer, he has illustrated many books on the Lakes and the North West.

Tony Drake is Footpath Secretary for RA Gloucestershire Area. He put forward the original idea of a footpath route along the Cotswold escarpment in the early 1950s, and has keenly championed it ever since.

Ken Piggin is a founder member of the Ebor Acorns, a York rambling club, and was their first Chairman. He originally conceived the idea of the Ebor Way for his club members, wrote the guide, and has since seen it become popular with walkers from far and wide.

David Sharp is Chairman of RA Southern Area. Through representing ramblers on the Towpaths Committee of the River Thames Society, he took up the cause of the Thames Walk and organised the Association's survey of the route.

Keith Thorrington was formerly a journalist on the Ramblers' Association office staff, who helped in preparing this book. Walking and reporting on Glyndwr's Way was his reward for services rendered!

Introduction

David Sharp

We met, by chance, on the riverside at Henley. My colleague heading homewards after a day in the office; my wife and I heading stationwards after a long and rewarding expedition. 'You mean you've walked . . . from Bourton on the Water!' He could be excused for finding it difficult to focus on the journey we were a few yards from completing. Bourton seemed very far away, indeed a whole county away, for our walk had crossed Oxfordshire. Perhaps in this day, when we think of travel in terms of climbing into a tin box, it needs some effort to believe that there remains a pleasant and appropriate way of making such an unlikely journey on foot, far from the roads and the sounds of civilisation. But there is, and while our inquisitor had spent the past few days behind a desk, we had spent them in another world and another time, following drove ways, Roman roads, ancient tracks, and the humble footpath ways, trod by our ancestors to link village communities. Perhaps it was only coming face to face with the twentieth century again, with the realisation that the mundane world had been going its own way while we went ours, that made us realise how effectively we had escaped. It brought a great conviction that our time had been better spent, walking the Oxfordshire Way.

This is just one of many such walks that have been established in recent years, and this book aims to introduce some of them and, incidentally, the people who created them. The concept of long-distance walks in this country began with the visionary idea put forward by Tom Stephenson in 1935, of a 'long green trail' from the Derbyshire Peak District to the Cheviots. Tom, secretary of the Ramblers' Association for many years, campaigned for his Pennine Way, and finally saw the legislation needed to create such routes embodied in the National Parks and Access to the Countryside Act of 1949. Even then, it was not until 1965 that the Pennine Way was formally opened, a tough and demanding 250 mile route that remains the best known of all the long treks, and the one that holds the most magnetic attraction to many walkers who see it as *the* challenge they must meet. The last weary miles over Windy Gyle and down into Kirk Yetholm over the Scottish border retain their sense of achievement, of elation in having overcome where less adventurous mortals have not even attempted.

Other routes have followed, and today the Countryside Commission has eleven such paths, the 'official' routes as they are termed, offering around 1,500 miles of walking. But while these government-approved projects were wending their laborious way to completion, there were many other lovers of our countryside who, inspired by Tom Stephenson's vision, saw green trails of their own as a means to introduce an area of much-loved country to others. So there came to develop a second and lesser network of ways, perhaps more truly the 'ramblers' ways' because ramblers thought of them, planned them and worked for their realisation. Many now have official status, in that enlightened county councils have adopted them. Wherever this has happened, we are indebted to county officers who have caught the same enthusiasm and provided extra help in signposting and negotiating.

It could be this very personal element of 'come and explore this land and love it as we do' that distinguishes our ramblers' ways from the others. This, and the fact that most (but not all) are easy, undemanding walks in quieter country where enjoyment is the theme rather than challenge. This book will tell little about peat bogs, but a great deal about woodland paths and sheltered villages, farmsteads and peaceful valleys. So these walks are for everyone to enjoy in their own way. You do not need seven-league boots, just the urge to explore in the one fashion that really suits the scale and subtlety of our English countryside —on foot.

These routes offer several advantages over setting out blindly. Firstly, ramblers have tried and experimented and finally chosen the best route with all their local knowledge to guide them. And of course they have described their route in a booklet or a map, or both. Secondly, although these walks use the many existing rights of way, most have been improved for your benefit, with signposts and a fine variety of waymarks to make the route clearer, obstructions removed, missing footbridges replaced, and stiles repaired. Thirdly, as a walk becomes more widely used, so the range of available accommodation grows, and even the village inn will come to expect a regular trade of ramblers. Several well-established routes offer accommodation lists as well as guides; the Cotswold Way, as an outstanding example, has a list originally compiled by canvassing of the local Womens' Institutes to find anyone able to put up a few wayfarers for the night. Now this very varied list is kept up-to-date by the recommendations of ramblers.

Unless we have speed records in mind, there are many ways to tackle these long-distance routes. Surely the most satisfying, though, is simply to plan the whole walk with overnight stops somewhere near the point where you feel you will have earned the rest. The village inn, a country farmhouse or even a humble cottage will give you that warm awareness of creature comfort awaiting you at the end of each day. Beyond doubt too, actually *staying* in a spot even for one night, talking over local affairs in the bar perhaps in the evening, gives you a sense of location, an awareness of being there rather than just passing through. So, even if you plan around leisurely spans of distance, regard 'the overnight stop as the way to enjoy the full flavour of a countryside.

Of course, the camper and the youth hosteller do something of the same thing, on a lower budget. The camping backpacker has the greatest freedom, but we must always hope that he asks permission first before settling on farming land. One irate farmer can take it out on everyone who follows along the walk. And do not discount hostelling on the idea that hostels are primitive or exclusively for an age group. You will find all manner and fashion of wayfarer staying in a hostel. They are graded today, even up to 'superior'; they can halve the cost of ordinary bed and breakfast and are in many ways better equipped to accommodate the walker, even to route advice from the warden.

Some walkers, particularly when they can organise themselves into a small, congenial party, prefer to follow a long-distance route from one or two convenient bases. The problem of getting to and from appropriate points on the route is then solved either by the services of a non-walking team-mate prepared to ferry the party back and forth by car, or even by hiring a minibus locally. It sounds expensive, but hire costs can be set against the convenience of staying exactly where you please.

Using the car presents a fundamental problem in that wherever you park it you must, sooner or later, return to it. On some routes this is a problem easily overcome by parking at the start of the day's walk and taking a bus back to it at the end of the day. The two-car formula is a far more subtle approach. You start with a party that can, with an acceptable level of temporary discomfort, squeeze into either of the two cars. Both cars drive to point A, where one is parked, the party climbs into the second car and proceeds to point B. Here the second car is parked and the whole party begins the day's walk, happy in the knowledge that when it reaches point A in the evening, the first car will be patiently waiting for them to pile in and return to point B, where they can disentangle themselves into two cars again. There are several permutations on this process, which sounds most complex but has the great advantage that, provided there is parking space, the two points can be chosen anywhere along the route that suits you.

The same variations are possible, using one car with a folding bicycle or two in the back. With your bicycle locked to a fence or traffic sign at one end of the walk, you park the car at the other end and walk to the bicycle with the aim of pedalling your way back to the car in the evening. It saves petrol, adds variety to your exercise, and of course even one individual can use this 'cycleback' technique. Connoisseurs arrange it so that the cycle ride is always downhill!

One further approach can be mentioned: simply treating the long journey as a sequence of single day walks. After all, there is no law that insists that a walk must be tackled as a continuous progress. Some of that special delight of the ramblers' way can be sampled just by trying a bit at a time, then returning next week or next month to take up where you left off. The Thames Walk with its excellent communications, is the outstanding example of the route that tempts you to explore in this fashion.

There is no special uniform to be worn when walking these ways. Some will take you over moorland or high mountain passes where weather can turn against you at any time of year, and shelter can be miles away. On these expeditions be sure to have good protective clothing for your safety's sake: a windproof anorak and a waterproof outer, some essential survival provisions, and extra woollies in case the temperature drops. But on the lowland walks these precautions are unnecessary, and water is the only element to worry about. With a planned itinerary to keep to, you cannot opt out of a day's walk just because the forecast says rain. So take really efficient rainwear and be prepared to carry on regardless. A waterproof cagoule or cape would be the popular choice, probably worn with waterproof over-trousers. And for footwear, boots should be worn on any walk where rough hill tracks will be hard on the ankles. Otherwise, sturdy, comfortable shoes will suffice along lowland field paths.

But whichever walk you set out on, take the published booklet or map as your essential and detailed guide. Take the 1:50 000 scale OS maps for the route too, for these will show you all the country around and identify distant landmarks—far more than just the narrow strip of route you are actually walking along. And if you do chance to wander from the described path, you will still be on the map and able to find your way back.

One last request—wherever you follow these ramblers' ways, remember the country code. When the routes were first planned, country people naturally wondered what trouble they would bring as visitors began to walk their little-used paths. Now they are reassured, as they realise we are the very best of countrygoers, passing quietly and considerately on our way without litter or open gates to be remembered by. Please try to enhance that reputation, and thus ensure a welcome for all the others who will come after you.

This book does not attempt to offer detailed route guidance; in every case there are lighter and handier little booklets to do this on your walk. Further, it can only select a representative range of walks. There are many more in England and Wales, and the only near-comprehensive guide is the *Fact Sheet No 2 on Long-Distance Paths*, published and updated regularly by the Ramblers' Association, 1/5 Wandsworth Road, London SW8 2LJ. It lists all the known routes, official and less official, the guide publications and where to obtain them. If you send for a copy, enclose a large addressed envelope and 25p postage.

The rest of the story can be left to our individual contributors. In most instances they are the pioneers and the inspiration behind the walk they write about. I hope they will inspire you to follow in their foot-steps. If you do, you will soon realise that others used these ways long before ramblers rediscovered them. The Romans, the drovers with their herds, the packhorse traders right back to prehistoric times—they also will be your companions as you cover the ground that they trod. The centuries make so little difference on the ramblers' ways. The countryside, once you get deep within it, has changed little, and our ways are ageless too.

The Dales Way

Colin Speakman

The Dales Way, one of the earliest of the 'unofficial' long-distance footpaths, is really rather an unusual kind of long-distance route. For most of its 81 miles it eschews the craggy tops or spectacular summit ridges, and keeps to valley bottoms. It is in essence a riverside route, or more accurately a linked series of riverside paths, crossing our third largest National Park, the Yorkshire Dales, in a south-east to north-west line. It connects the edge of an urban fringe, the dormitory town of Ilkley, to the shores of England's largest lake, Windermere—and of course the very special magic of the Lake District National Park.

Maybe that is why the Dales Way is such an attraction. It is certainly not the longest, the wildest or even the grandest of our paths, but by common consent one of the most beautiful. There are the contrasts of its river scenery, with beauty succeeding beauty. The northbound walker has that romantic image as his goal—the Lakeland peaks and shimmering waters; and behind him the mills, factories and offices of bustling, urban England.

So, perhaps not surprisingly, the Dales Way has secured a very high place in the affections of many walkers, experienced and less experienced alike. epitomising as it does all that is best of the Yorkshire Dales —the magnificence of the limestone scenery, the unspoiled beauty of the villages, the grandeur of the fells, and the subtle contrasts and quiet charm of such areas as Dentdale or Bolton Abbey.

But there are other, more pragmatic reasons for the Dales Way's popularity. It is an easy route. There is only one short section of real fell country where, without boots and a compass, the going on a bad day can be tough. For the most part it is easy, even gentle walking, the rate of ascent or descent merely that of a river's making. It can easily be fitted into a short holiday—a week is more than ample—so can form a

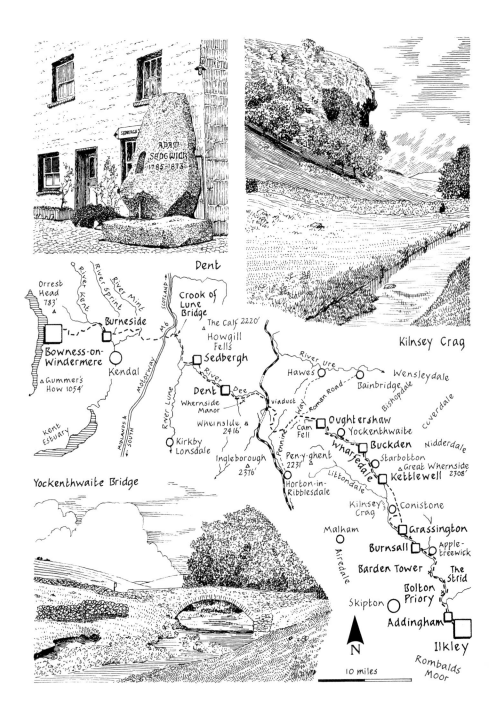

Dent

Kilnsey Crag

Yockenthwaite Bridge

delightful spring or autumn holiday, a pleasant second holiday that does not use up too much time or resources. It also keeps, with rare exception, to the natural ways of communication. Dales have shops, friendly pubs, farmhouses, charming villages and even, if you are not so conditioned to the inside of a motor car that you cannot read a bus timetable any longer, a surprisingly good supply of country bus and even train services, including, in the summer months, the celebrated Dales Rail service and the new Three Peaks bus service which make it easy to walk the Dales Way in stages. Or for that matter a welcome respite should climate and blisters sour the delights of riverside footpaths.

Maybe the best thing of all is that the Dales Way walker is not secluded from civilisation on remote and windy heights. Great country is not just a backcloth—it has a human dimension. And the Dales Way reflects the character of the Dales people. Like the landscape they are tough, independent, individualists, with a remarkable sense of hospitality and a way of life which reflects a continuity that has lasted for centuries. To understand just a little of this way of life, whether just observing the seasonal work on the upland farms, or spending a night in a Dales farmhouse, is to share this experience, and this is as much a part of the Dales Way as the magnificent views and almost perfect landscapes which the walker can enjoy.

The Dales Way has a somewhat curious history. It began as a great but simple idea in the mind of Tom Wilcock, Footpath Secretary for the Ramblers' Association's West Riding Area. Tom's idea was that there should be a right of way alongside every single river in the Yorkshire Dales. This was in the mid-1960s, soon after the old West Riding County Council definitive footpath map had been finalised and many obvious gaps in the region's footpath system were evident.

When the county council was approached, their Deputy County Planning Officer proved sympathetic, but gave the Ramblers some sound advice. This was to be realistic, and instead of having paths by every river, to select the most important as a priority.

Wharfedale was an obvious choice. The longest and most majestic of the Yorkshire Dales, beloved by generations of writers, artists and ramblers, already had excellent riverside paths on the footpath map.

Only a few gaps remained to be completed. But a Wharfedale path has one obvious drawback. If you followed the Wharfe from Ilkley to its source, where did it take you? The answer was a bog—a bleak moor high on Cam Fell where the Wharfe peters out into a series of sikes and drains. No, something more was required, something to give the path some glamour, some purpose.

Not far over the Cam Fell watershed, the headwaters of the River Dee rise, forming the infant Dentdale, one of the most intimately beautiful of all the dales, contrasting dramatically with the more grandiose splendours of Wharfedale. So a Wharfe–Dee path became a possibility with Sedbergh as a target, and the rest followed naturally. Why not, having got to Sedbergh, follow the Lune northwards alongside those ancient Howgill Fells, cutting across the low Westmorland hills by the rivers Mint and Kent to the Lake District itself?

The Ramblers were quick to gain the support of the old West Riding Committee of the Yorkshire Dales National Park (the Park then being divided between two county councils) and the Westmorland County Council Planning Officer offered a number of suggestions about the final section of route into Bowness. So, hoping that the Dales Way would soon be declared 'official', the Countryside Commission were approached.

Surprisingly, the Commission were less than enthusiastic. It later turned out that they were planning their own high-level spur from the Pennine Way to the Lake District via the Howgill Fells and southern Borrowdale which, though it went through spectacular scenery, touched no human habitation and was therefore somewhat lacking in such creature comforts as most mortals tend to require. But equally, protracted legal battles over short stretches of long-distance paths elsewhere in the country seemed to have sapped the strength and will of the Commission to accept any new routes.

Undeterred, the West Riding Ramblers decided that the idea was too good to be allowed to die. Articles were written, the local press involved, and on a celebrated day in 1969 a party of 126 arrived outside the post office in Ilkley for an unofficial inaugural tramp to Barden. At the end of that walk, the local bus company had to operate a shuttle service to ferry the walkers back to Ilkley.

The Dalesman Publishing Company, that unsung champion of the unofficial long-distance path, published the first guidebook to the route, narrowly beating a rival from Gerrards of Nelson, and the Dales Way was born.

People create paths, not officials. Harassed bureaucrats, whose view of a footpath is generally from a car window, do not determine the rich pattern of our heritage. Boots trace the way, bend the bracken, flatten the turf. And so it was with the Dales Way.

To be fair, a decade after that first splendid inauguration, the Countryside Commission repented of their sins and have now indicated through their newly established Yorkshire region, that the Dales Way may receive formal recognition as a Recreational Footpath. Both Bradford Metropolitan District Council and the Yorkshire Dales National Park Authority are giving priority to the waymarking of the route, including the erection of signs with the coveted Dales Way insignia, and it is likely that South Lakeland District Council and the Lake District National Park will soon follow suit. To their lasting credit, West Yorkshire County Council have actually created a new section of footpath, the first new piece of Dales Way—albeit over their own land—at Fairfield, north of Addingham. It is a small but significant step in the right direction. Whether other authorities along the Way are prepared to follow this example is another question.

Geology and natural history

Rocks make a landscape. The geology of the Dales Way is contained within two major geological epochs—Carboniferous and Silurian. The Carboniferous contains a number of dramatically contrasting rock types. There are the gritstones and sandstones of mid-Wharfedale, the heather moors and dark gritty outcrops of Beamsley Beacon, Simon Seat and Barden Moor that dominate the first part of the walk. Then, around Appletreewick, is the sudden transition to pale limestones, the great dome-like reef knolls above Appletreewick and Thorpe, the Great Scar limestones that are exposed where the Craven Fault crosses the Wharfe at Linton Falls, and the beautiful, exposed terraces of the Yoredale limestones above Kettlewell and into Langstrothdale.

Dentdale, followed by the Dales Way, with the Howgill Fells in the distance
(*Yorkshire Dales National Park*)

The top of the dale leads back to the boulder clays and acid, peaty moorlands of Cam and Newby Head, before the deep chasm of the Dee again cuts through to limestone, this time the unusual, black limestones of Dentdale, with its river vanishing underground for hundreds of yards before surfacing through such strange natural caverns as those at Hell's Cauldron near Gibb's Hall.

From Sedbergh there is a major change in the rock structure to the far older Silurian Slates, typical of much of the Lake District. The change is marked by the Dent Fault which crosses the lower part of Dentdale in the vicinity of Gawthrop. The landscape, the drystone walls, the farmhouses now take on a Lake District flavour, with this section of the Dales Way dominated by the smooth, green, dome-like summits of the Howgill Fells. The upper parts of Lunedale and the Lune Gorge, now shared by river, railway and motorway, again have a quite different character, with the deceptively gentle country beyond the Lune finally yielding to the gnarled, spiky summits of the south western fells and the great natural canyon that contains Windermere itself.

The wildlife to be seen on the Dales Way is rich and varied. The riversides are the haunt of a wide range of birdlife, including dippers, wagtails, martins, swallows, and, on occasions, the spectacular king-fisher. The Wharfe in particular is a famous trout river, with brown trout leaping clear of the water after flies on quiet summer days.

On the higher moorlands, the curlew is often the walker's companion as is the golden plover, the heron and the oyster catcher and, from some of the higher rocky edges, the kestrel or even buzzard or other bird of prey. Smaller mammals will also be in evidence—hares, the occasional fox, stoats, and voles.

But perhaps the particular glory of the Dales Way lies in the wild flowers to be seen in late spring and early summer. Primroses, violets and cowslips are still to be found in profusion, as are the wood anemone, ragged robin, bluebell, campion, ramsons, kingcup, musk and, on the higher limestone terraces, the beautiful bird's eye primrose, the mountain pansy, rock roses and scented thymes.

Farming, in particular sheep farming, also offers much to interest the observant rambler, with a marked contrast between the relative lowlands in the lower parts of Wharfedale or west of the Lune, and the sparse, wild country above Langstrothdale and Cam, where spring comes late and winter early, and economic survival is difficult. The breeds of sheep contrast, with the familiar black-faced Swaledale and Dales-bred sheep of the Yorkshire Dales, and the Herdwicks of the Lakeland fells.

For convenience, the Dales Way has been subdivided into seven day stages based either on available public transport or accommodation, which will need to be modified to meet individual requirements.

Ilkley to Barden

The Dales Way commences its 81 mile journey at the seventeenth-century bridge in Ilkley, some 200yd west of the present bridge over the Wharfe. A tarmac path goes by allotments and tennis courts before becoming a field path, marked by metal kissing gates, which reaches the old road to Addingham, to follow the riverside to the former textile mills at Low Addingham. The route passes a series of early nineteenth-century cottages to reach Addingham Church, and, just skirting the modern commuter village, keeps by the riverside from the suspension bridge to a second mill.

Under the shadow of Beamsley Beacon, the Dales Way now follows the riverside to Fairfield Cottage to connect with the new section of right of way (not on most ordnance survey maps), following the long curve of the riverside by parkland to Fairfield Hall.

A short stretch of road walking along the busy and dangerous B6160 road (footpath creations required) before a link path leads to Bolton Bridge; and now the Dales Way enters the Yorkshire Dales National Park along a stretch of riverside path frequented by Wordsworth, Turner and Ruskin, to one of the most famous and picturesque ruins in England, Bolton Priory, which was an Augustinian foundation.

Burnsall in Wharfedale. The Dales Way crosses the bridge over the Wharfe
(*Yorkshire Dales National Park*)

Crossing the Wharfe by footbridge or stepping stones, the Dales Way enters Bolton Park by a path which is not a right of way and for which a small toll is payable, taking the walker to a wooden bridge that leads to the Cavendish Pavilion (open daily from spring to autumn for meals and light refreshments; weekends in winter). The Way returns to the east side of the river to follow the path through lush, romantic woodlands to the Strid, where rocky ledges squeeze the Wharfe into a swirling, narrow torrent. It is a thrilling and terrifying spot, with its many tales of death by drowning, from the twelfth-century 'Boy of Egremont' to recent victims who still cannot resist attempting the treacherous leap. Then it continues past the ornate Bradford Water-works viaduct, carrying aqueducts from Nidderdale, to reach the seventeenth-century Barden Bridge, one of the most beautiful of all the bridges over the Wharfe. Across the bridge and up the hill is the fifteenth-century Barden Tower, home of the Shepherd Lord, the legendary 10th Lord Clifford who, in fear of his life during the Wars of the Roses, was brought up as a common shepherd boy in the hills of Cumberland.

Barden to Grassington

A pleasant stretch of riverside leads to Howgill under the shadow of Simon Seat, one of the most popular of the smaller Dales peaks and a noted viewpoint, now part of the Barden Fell Access Area. Returning to the river, the Dales Way follows a narrow, wooded path above rapids and through an attractive wooded glen before emerging below Appletreewick, a Dales village with campsites and a couple of pubs. The riverside path leads on to Burnsall, rightly regarded as a village with an incomparably lovely setting in a vast bowl of hills. Its riverside village green, church with Viking gravestones, seventeenth-century school, cafe and inn make it a welcome port of call.

Continuing behind the Red Lion Inn, the path goes by Loup Scar, a fine exposure of limestone, to the little suspension bridge below Hebden, built towards the end of the last century by the local black-smith. Now follows a gentle section of riverside by a long avenue of chestnuts, until the Norman church at Linton comes into view, acces-sible from the Dales Way by stepping stones when the river is low. The path winds by the ancient manorial corn mill, now converted into dwellings, to the majestic falls at Linton Mill and the bridge at Grassington.

Grassington, the principal village of Upper Wharfedale, makes a natural centre for the Dales Way. A busy township which has nonetheless kept its character, it is well supplied with most conveniences of civilisation, including a good range of shops, pubs, cafes, an excellent local museum and a National Park Centre by the car park. Staff at the Centre welcome Dales Way walkers who call, and both the Centre and the Dales Book Shop in the village are well supplied with maps and guides of the area, and of the Dales Way in particular.

Grassington to Buckden

From Grassington, the notion of following the Wharfe northwards suffers a slight setback. A superb stretch of riverside path leads by Ghaistrills Strid to Grass Wood, but beyond the wood no right of way exists. It is therefore essential to take a high-level path from Grassington via Town Head Farm and up to Lea Green—itself an area full of ancient archaeological remains in the form of Celtic fields and early mine workings—to take a dramatically beautiful path across the limestones of Conistone Old Pasture and Conistone Dib to Hill Castle Scar. The Way then threads along the narrow terraces opposite the great bulk of Kilnsey Crag, looking down Littondale, before descending by the almost Scandinavian-roofed Church of England Residential Centre at Scar Gill. A choice of field paths leads into Kettlewell.

Kettlewell, a former mining village, is another natural centre for Dales Wayfarers with a youth hostel, inns, cafes, and a couple of shops. The path continues at the far side of the river, now keeping close to the riverside past Starbotton (connected by footbridge and stepping stones), the valley steeper now and the river swifter flowing.

Buckden is reached through an area of surprisingly exotic parkland and woodland, following the floodbank to Buckden Bridge. A smaller centre than Kettlewell, it nonetheless has an inn, cafes, a shop, and, as the terminus of the Upper Wharfedale bus, an excellent point to start or finish a day on the Dales Way.

The Dales Way descending into the valley near Scar Gill House
(*Geoffrey Berry*)

Buckden to Denthead

This is the longest and toughest section of the Dales Way, since it requires some genuine fellwalking. The first section is easy and delightful enough, following the riverside path almost to Hubberholme, with its George Inn and Church with a rare rood-loft screen, relic of pre-Reformation days. Through Yockenthwaite to Deepdale and Beckermonds before being forced to join the metalled road to Oughtershaw, the Way is gentle enough. But leaving Oughtershaw, a veritable last outpost of civilisation, by way of Swarthgill, the walking is a tough and wild transition from track to moorland path.

Cam Houses offers some respite for the walker with refreshments at the farm and accommodation available in the new Bunkhouse Barn (*see* table) before the ascent through the edge of woodland to the Dales Way Cairn high on Cam End, where for a short distance the Dales Way and the Pennine Way meet. The Dales Way then descends to ford the infant Ribble above Gearstones, to cross the main B6479 Ingleton–Hawes road.

The Dales Way now turns north via Winshaw, High Gayle and the bleak edge of Stoops Moss to Newby Head before descending the Dentdale road to Denthead—graced by a youth hostel and, a little further north, an inn.

Denthead to Sedbergh

Dentdale is pure joy—its winding, cascading river frequently vanishing out of sight, the hedgerows creamy white with blackthorn in the spring.

From Lea Yeat a short stretch of riverside path runs to Ewegales, then, with care, the winding hillside path to Little Town, Hacker Gill and Clint can be traced before crossing the river at Nelly Brig and taking the riverside path to Tommy Brig. Directly opposite is Whernside Cave and Fell Centre, a former eighteenth-century plantation owner's house, now owned by the Yorkshire Dales National Park Committee. Overnight accommodation, limited camping and equipment are available at the Centre and Dales Way walkers are welcome. Returning to Mill Bridge, the Way follows Deepdale Beck to its confluence with the Dee, then to Church Bridge and Dent village with its cobbles and unspoiled centre at the huge fountain of Shap granite erected to the memory of Adam Sedgwick, the great Victorian geologist, born in Dent.

From Dent, the riverside path continues to Barth Bridge and, keeping to the same side of the river, to Dillicar. The Dales Way utilises a narrow grass-grown lane, distinguished by splendid hedgerows, to Rash Bridge, before crossing the river and taking a field path that climbs to join the ancient bridleway over the edge of Long Rigg to Millthrop. Here is one of the most splendid viewpoints of the Dales Way, overlooking the township of Sedbergh set against a magnificent backcloth of the Howgill Fells.

Sedbergh, dominated by its famous public school, offers all the facilities of a pleasant small town. The National Park Centre in Joss Lane carries a display of local information, including an interpretation of the countryside around Sedbergh.

Sedbergh to Burneside

From Millthrop Bridge on the Dent road, the Dales Way follows a new river, the Rawthey, keeping to a riverside of rocky splendour, soon passing its confluence with the Dee. The little Quaker meeting house at Brigflatts just off the Dales Way is well worth a visit, an important early relic of the birth of Quakerism which owes much to the inspiration of a great oration given by George Fox on nearby Firbank Fell in 1652.

The Dales Way crosses the A683 and descends to the River Lune by the old farm of High Oaks, following Lunedale northwards beyond the A684 and the derelict cast-iron bridge that once carried the Ingleton–Tebay railway. The Way now leaves the riverside, tracing old tracks between old farms to Bramaskew, Nether Bainbridge and Hole House, before returning to a fine stretch of riverside.

The sixteenth-century Crook of Lune bridge, over which the Dales Way passes
(*Geoffrey Berry*)

The narrow hump-backed bridge at Crook of Lune marks the exit from the Yorkshire Dales National Park—under the huge, abandoned viaduct of red brick at Lowgill, and then to meet the West Coast electrified main line railway and the noise of the M6 just beyond Beckfoot, *en route* to Lambrigg Head.

Parkland and pleasant pastoral country, with scattered woodlands and the first arable fields of the Dales Way, now dominate the route. Path finding needs care here, cutting behind Holme Park and then in front of Moresdale Hall, by Hardrigg to Grayrigg Foot, Shaw End and Biglands, and Black Moss Tarn.

Burneside Hall

A lane leads past Skelsmergh Tarn to the A6, quieter since the M6 now takes the bulk of Anglo-Scottish traffic. By Burton Farm and Oakbank, the Dales Way crosses the little River Sprint at Sprint Mill to enter Burneside by Burneside Hall, a fortified pele tower, grim reminder of the days when the Scottish border reivers terrorised the northern counties in the late Middle Ages.

Burneside has limited accommodation and facilities, but is a short train or bus ride from Kendal or no more than a 2 mile walk mainly by riverside. Kendal is a major centre with a youth hostel and ample comforts to console the tiredest walker.

Burneside to Bowness

The final stage of the Dales Way is no anticlimax and possesses splendours of its own. Initially the riverside path along the Kent from Burneside is tame enough, but beyond Cowen Head where the river is crossed, it becomes a scramble over craggy embankments before entering Staveley, a pleasant and compact town just within the Lake District National Park.

Tracks and lanes bring the Dales Way past New Hall to Waingap before climbing up to Crag House and Outrun Nook, and to one of the most thrilling moments of the whole 81 miles. The path winds between the craggy knolls on the side of Grandsire, curving round between heather to give a sudden glorious view of the whole expanse of the Lakeland fells with Windermere below in the great chasm between the hills.

After such a moment, the closing stages of the Dales Way can only be a coda—Cleabarrow, Matson Ground and due westwards through the woods by Brant Fell to an enclosed track which leads to the centre of Bowness and, directly ahead, the glittering expanse of Windermere.

Bowness is a busy tourist centre with ample facilities. A regular bus service from the promenade runs to Windermere Station from where a railcar service links the town with Oxenholme and the West Coast main line.

Short Walks along the Dales Way

The Wharfedale section of the Dales Way is particularly well suited for walkers doing the route in sections, because of the excellent public transport facilities. The through rail-bus Parklink Wharfedale ticket gives direct access from many west Yorkshire towns by rail to Skipton and then by bus to Bolton Abbey, Grassington or Buckden or any intermediate point. Many excellent short walks along the Dales Way, some of them circular, are indicated in a booklet *Parklink Walks in Upper Wharfedale*. The Dalesrider bus-only ticket is also of great value, allowing the rambler to return from an outward point by bus. By using the large public car parks at Bolton Abbey, Burnsall, Grassington, Kettlewell or Buckden, a walker can plan his ramble to utilise public transport back to his parked vehicle, thus making the most of the service.

The central sections of the Dales Way are more difficult to do in short sections, but in summer months the Dales Rail service from Ribblehead and Dent Stations, and use of either D. W. Whaites Settle–Ribblehead–Hawes bus or J. R. Woof's Dentdale minibus service, both forming part of the Yorkshire Dales National Park's Three Peaks Bus Service, enable the area between Buckden and Dent to be conveniently covered.

The Ribble service from Kendal to Sedbergh and a late afternoon bus along the A685 from Grayrigg to Kendal (weekdays only) make the Lunedale section of the Dales Way possible with careful planning from Kendal, whilst the paytrain service from Kendal to Burneside, Staveley and Windermere, as well as regular bus services along the A591, make the final stretch of the Dales Way among the easiest and most accessible sections for the walker undertaking the route in stages.

The Dales Way

Progressive Mileage	Miles Between	Places on route	Bus service to	Rail Service	Cafes	Accommodation	Inns providing snacks etc	Shops	Camping
-	-	Ilkley	Harrogate, Otley, Skipton etc.	●	●	●	●	●	
3	3	Addingham	as above	●			●	●	
6	3	Bolton Abbey	Ilkley, Skipton, Grassington		●	●		●	
12	6	Barden	as above		●				●
16	4	Burnsall	as above		●	●	●	●	
19	3	Grassington	as above		●	●	●	●	
26	7	Kettlewell	Grassington, Skipton		●	●	●	●	
29	3	Starbotton	as above				●		
31	2	Buckden	as above			●	●	●	Official sites only
37	6	Oughtershaw	—						
41	4	Cam Houses	—			●			
44	3	Gearstones	Hawes, Settle (Tu. Sat. Sun. summer only)	DR			●		●
47	3	Denthead	—	DR	●	●	●	●	●
52	5	Dent	Kendal Sedburgh	DR	●	●	●	●	●
58	6	Sedbergh	Kendal, Hawes Tu. Fri.	DR	●	●	●	●	●
64	6	Beckfoot	—						
69	5	Grayrigg Foot	Kendal, Tebay			●	●		
73	4	Burneside	Kendal, Windermere	●	●	●	●	●	
76	3	Staveley	as above	●	●	●	●	●	
81	5	Bowness	Windermere	●	●	●	●	●	●

DR — Dales Rail service from Dent and Ribblehead stations on certain weekends only

There are youth hostels at Linton, Kettlewell, Denthead and Kendal

Early closing: Tuesday afternoon at Kettlewell, Wednesday at Ilkley, Thursday at Grassington, Sedbergh, Kendal and Windermere

Camping Barns: There are experimental camping barns at Cam Houses and Cat Holes (Sedbergh). Details from National Park Office, Hedben Road, Grassington, Skipton, N. Yorkshire

The Three Forests Way

Fred Matthews

Nowhere does the countryside come so close to London as Epping Forest, its nearest point within half a dozen miles of the City of London itself. The remaining forest is a remnant of the Great Forest of Waltham which covered the whole of southern Essex as far as Great Dunmow, and included what are now Hatfield and Hainault Forests. So today, three areas remain of the ancient hunting forest, with between them the low rolling hills of Essex; wide open skies and open pastoral landscapes with reminders of the past in the fine weather-boarded cottages and farmsteads, and an occasional name like Little Forest Hall. Here once was all woodland.

In 1976 was born the concept of a circular footpath route linking the three forests. It would be some 60 miles long, starting and ending at Loughton, the nearest point to London, but which could be joined anywhere along the route in fine country which is surprisingly never more than 35 miles from the centre of the capital. The route was surveyed by members of the West Essex Group of the Ramblers' Association, and opened by them on an inaugural walk over the three days of August bank holiday 1977, a rambling commemoration of Her Majesty's Silver Jubilee.

Despite the name, the route passes mainly through open countryside and the forest sections total only some eight miles. But all three forests have open public access, so as you reach them you can turn aside and explore at will. Taken in the more usual direction, the walk starts through Epping Forest, a mere 15 minute uphill pull after leaving Loughton station on the Central Line. The present forest covers 6,000 acres, stretching from Forest Gate to Epping with a detached section beyond, a total length of over 12 miles. It was saved for public enjoyment by the Corporation of the City of London, supported by the

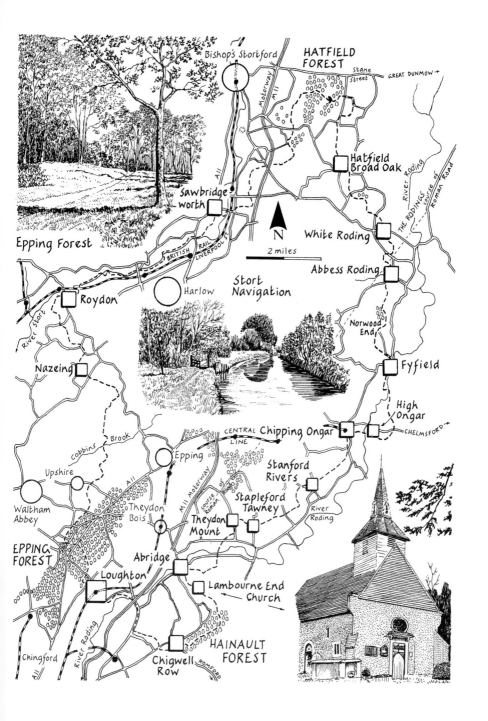

Bishop's Stortford

HATFIELD FOREST

Stane Street

GREAT DUNMOW →

M11 Motorway

Hatfield Broad Oak

Epping Forest

Sawbridge worth

A11

BRITISH RAIL LIVERPOOL

N

2 miles

White Roding

THE RODINGS

course of Roman Road

RIVER RODING

Abbess Roding

Stort Navigation

Harlow

Roydon

River Stort

Nazeing

Norwood End

Fyfield

High Ongar

Cobbins Brook

CENTRAL LINE

Chipping Ongar

CHELMSFORD

Upshire

Epping

A11

M11 Motorway

course of Roman

Stanford Rivers

Stapleford Tawney

River Roding

Waltham Abbey

Theydon Bois

Theydon Mount

EPPING FOREST

Abridge

Loughton

Lambourne End Church

Chingford

A11

River Roding

ROMFORD

Chigwell Row

HAINAULT FOREST

Commons Preservation Society, in Victorian times. To the south, the forest keeps reminding us of its urban surroundings, but these soon fade from view and here at Loughton we can plunge into the true forest of beech, hornbeam and silver birch. The ground is mainly boulder clay with some outcrops of sand, and characteristic of the forest are the many delightful ponds and streams beneath the trees with their carpet of fallen leaves shining a golden brown underfoot for most of the year. It is advisable to wear stout footwear here, and beware of walking on the darker patches of leaves which conceal wet and boggy areas.

The broad, main track we turn onto after entering the forest just short of the sandy Strawberry Hill Pond, will soon take us past another delightful pond, the Earls Path Pond, home of ducks and irises. After dropping a little muddily into a valley with a stream at its foot, we are soon climbing the escarpment of ancient Loughton Camp. Although the trees have now taken over, the circular outline of the camp can easily be traced as a raised rampart with a surrounding ditch. Two thousand years ago it would have held a good defensive position on its steep slope 100ft above the valleys of Kate's Cellar and Debden Slade. Today it is an eerie spot with its gnarled old trees. Over the busy A11, the walk comes to the best-known spot in the whole forest, High Beech or Beach. Opinions differ on the name; some spell it Beech after the trees, and some Beach after the sand layer that comes to the surface here. At this spot Queen Victoria declared the forest open after the passing of the Epping Forest Act of 1878. Now the Epping Forest Conservation Centre stands here, well worth a visit for its frequently changing exhibitions on many aspects of the forest. Away westward, the view so beloved of Londoners is now closed in by trees, but glimpses remain over the Lea valley.

Now the route follows one of the old forest ways, the Verderers' Ride, along the ridge to Honey Lane where we leave Epping Forest. Many will regret having to leave it so soon. At all times and seasons it makes pleasant walking—in early morning with sunlight touching

Along the Verderers' Ride through Epping Forest (*David Sharp*)

early spring leaves or autumn colours, evening light filtered over the forest ponds, or the pristine whiteness of occasional winter snows. Sad too that the deer have now mainly left for the sanctuary at Theydon Bois to the south-east of the forest. Hopefully though, if the wind is north, we will see deer as we walk on to Epping Green. On this section we follow part of the 20 mile Forest Way which offers an alternative route between Epping and Hatfield Forests. Essex County Council has waymarked it with oak posts and Forest Way plaques. Passing by a charming duckpond, it enters the Warlies Estate, recently purchased by the Greater London Council partly for use as a country park. Combined with Epping Forest and the 21 mile long Lea Valley Regional Park, to the west, this area will soon be remarkably well endowed with public open space. On the track to little Upshire hamlet, we can see on our right the dark edge of the forest, and to our left a view where, on a clear day, you can even tell the time by distant Waltham Abbey clock.

Beyond Upshire is Copt Hall Green, a tiny detached part of Epping Forest. These detached areas date back to the Epping Forest Act when all common land in Epping parish was declared to be part of the forest. Now comes the first taste of open Essex countryside as the path drops to the vale of Cobbins Brook, then climbs past old Parvilles Farm to the wide grassy ride of Epping Long Green, another detached part of the forest. The ride provides us with a ridge walk along to Epping Green itself, where the Forest Way leaves us to follow its own route south of Harlow. We turn to take paths on to Nazeing Common, with views to our left that are more reminiscent of the Adur valley in Sussex than anywhere in Essex. As we tramp down the green lane to the Sun pub at Nazeing Common, we are following part of a network of some 400 miles of these ways in Essex; the old roads that have never been surfaced. Over the years many have become overgrown and impassable, but this is just one example that has been cleared and brought back into use by Ramblers' Association working parties. They are delightful in summer, providing a shady walk and a home for so many birds and for primroses, violets and even wild orchids deeper into Essex.

Beyond Nazeing church on its low hill, the walk takes us to the top of a ridge with views over the Lea valley that are impressive if somewhat industrialised, and reveal just how this river has saved Essex from

Along the river Stort between Roydon and Harlow
(*David Sharp*)

the untidy development on the Hertfordshire bank. After the ridge,
the route drops steeply down a wooded slope and past a pretty little
lock-keeper's cottage to the Stort Navigation. The towpath is followed
for some five miles now, a surprising walk passing to the north of
Harlow New Town with industry often nearby, but somehow the
navigation keeps its rural character and the occasional long boats add
the romance of a different century.

At Sawbridgeworth we are just on the Hertfordshire border, and
a deviation is worthwhile to visit the town and particularly the area
around the church. Otherwise we leave the navigation here with a
third of our circuit completed, to head for Hatfield Forest. Now there
are wide skyscapes and open views again, as for a while the countryside
becomes more arable. With the disappearance of many hedges, some
big fields are crossed, but mainly the Way follows good headland paths
and green lanes out to Woodside Green, owned by the National Trust
and abutting on to Hatfield Forest. We do not plunge immediately
into the forest but choose a quieter way by field edge and tracks beside
woods to enter above the lake.

Hatfield Forest covers around 1,000 acres today, with areas of hornbeam and oak, and several fine open belts of parkland. At its centre, the lake and its adjoining marsh harbour mallard, teal, waterhen and snipe, overlooked by the shell house built by the Houblon family in 1759. Now it houses a very welcome refreshment kiosk and a National Trust information centre that tells of their policies in renewing the forest coppices. Leaving the forest we start on the remotest leg of the walk, southwards now to follow the Princey Brook through its water-meadows. Here the flora is mainly large thistles, but the area is alight with summer colour from the many butterflies that live by the brook.

The Three Forests Way passes a fine Essex church at Hatfield Broad Oak
(*D. H. Goodwin*)

Climbing from the stream to Hatfield Broad Oak, we are precisely half way around our circuit. This is one of the larger villages and well worth exploring. Especially fine is the street of typical Essex village houses that the Way passes through. As you walk the footpaths of this parish you will be sure to notice the large and unusual waymark stones that guide you. They were placed in position by the late Councillor Lumley—the preservation of the footpaths in this area owes a great deal to the dedication of this true country-lover.

The tracks on to White Roding are very fine, but alas also used by horseriders, so that they can be somewhat churned up and muddy. Soon we will meet the Roding itself, the river that gives its name to the eight, or some say nine, villages of the Roding country. Abbess, Aythorpe with its windmill, Berners with its tiny church, Beauchamp, High, Leaden, Margaret on the delightful lanes leading to the Easters, White and the ninth, the legendary Morrell Roding of which few traces remain. The Roding was renowned for its watermeadows which were a sea of summer flowers, but the advance of the wheatfields has caught up with them and between White Roding and Ongar our walk crosses many an arable field. But the villages remain, peaceful and largely unchanged down their lanes with verges a mass of Queen Anne's lace in early summer and later of meadowsweet, while deep in the Roding country the roadside ditches will be covered in primroses, violets and in some parts cowslips. Where hedges remain, sadly not as many as there used to be, dog rose and honeysuckle enhance the way.

This is an enchanting part of England, just 20 miles from London. Or a lifetime from London; distances to towns have no significance in these rural places. The low hills give just enough climbing to provide the long rolling Essex views, and a wide blue bowl of crystal-clear air tempered with a light breeze will wave the corn like ripples of the sea.

The arable fields of clay can be heavy going when ploughed in late autumn and early winter, but when harrowed and sown the walking conditions improve, the more so as the path is walked back by our own feet. In the larger fields it is necessary to walk the right of way through the crops, but keeping in single file takes up only a foot or so in width, there is no great loss of crop and detouring round a large, sown field is not a practical proposition on a walk of any length.

Our Way passes through three of the Roding villages. The next, Abbess Roding, has a fine church and just before it a very attractive farmhouse viewed over its duckpond. Continuing over undulating hills, the view to the left is to my favourite Essex church, Beauchamp Roding. It stands, isolated but not lonely, always framed against the vast open sky. Soon at Norwood End we meet up with another long-distance walk, the Essex Way. With it we traverse a ridge with wooded valleys around us and primroses and violets by the enchanting and easy-going track down to Fyfield. Here a path leads to our first crossing of the Roding and a spot to linger at. The little river is a mass of water-lilies with mallard, coot and teal pushing their way through. The water edge is fringed with purple loosestrife, meadowsweet and reeds. Past Fyfield church the Way recrosses the river with glimpses down to pretty Fyfield Mill, then starts down the valley to cross the Roding yet again at the quaintly named Tun Bridge. On a warm day it is pleasant to stand on the bridge and watch the fish passing beneath. For the amount of water in the river, the size of the roach and pike is quite surprising. Now following the bank where sweet rocket grows, the path climbs to Little Forest Hall, then on with valley views to High Ongar and Ongar itself.

A stroll down Ongar High Street is a worthwhile diversion. With its very English mix of old and new, this street is now a conservation area and at night you might admire its experimental lighting of a lemon shade, giving an impression of moonlight. This has been developed for conservation areas and could be adopted generally in place of the glaring orange that floods so many of our towns and villages. The church is to the left of the High Street, and a path to the left and beyond it will take you past the mound and moat of the old castle site. On the town side was a courtyard with an 80ft wide rampart, and beyond this a rampart has been traced which embraced what was then the whole of the town of Ongar. Apart from its history, Ongar is now an important walkers' centre, as it is also on the 65 mile Essex Way path from Epping to Dedham, and on the St Peter's Way, a 45 mile route to St Peter's-on-the-Wall, Bradwell, opened in 1978 by West Essex RA Group. It is thus on three long-distance path routes, as well as being the terminus of the Central Line!

Onward, the walk takes a path strangely named 'Kettlebury' to Stanford Rivers, then by a cleared green lane in the direction of Stapleford Tawney. With the Roding valley opening up before us, the far distant and often misty views are to the City of London. Ahead are the fine buildings of the farm on the site of Great Tawney Hall, and we turn down to Stapleford Tawney church. In the churchyard the chionodoxa shines as a sea of blue around the entrance gate in spring, and the little church with its shingled Essex spire looks over the valley to its equally lonely sister church of Theydon Mount. Both churches are good viewpoints and we take the church path over the valley that links them. The route drops to cross the Roding again, then via the woodlands of Apes Grove, a mass of bluebells in spring, into Abridge village. Here the old buildings, several groups of sixteenth-century origin amongst them, are grouped around the market square.

At Lambourne End on the Way, a remote little part-Norman church (*D. H. Goodwin*)

The path that climbs from Abridge leads to Lambourne church, the family church of the Lockwood family. There are low Norman doorways to the side and a mural found when restoration work was being done. Beyond the church looking back, there is a panoramic view from Epping Forest and Epping via Ongar Park Wood to Ongar and south to Kelvedon Hatch, the countryside we have travelled through. The bridle-path from here on leads to the fine weather-boarded Church House with a pond and many bullrushes, then on as a green lane, Featherbed Lane. This lane too has been cleared by West Essex Group RA members, and makes a fine approach to Hainault Forest. These old lanes can often be linked together on the map and their past significance guessed at. This one appears to have formed part of the road that led from Epping to Romford.

Hainault is the smallest of our three forests, but the most rural as there are no roads through it, or cars allowed in it. In spring some of the tracks can be wet but they can be bypassed by walking in the trees beside the path. The open space on top of the hill we come to was once a junction of trackways, and here it was that our old Epping to Romford road turned south-east to Collier Row. Flora is scarce in the forest apart from bramble. There are primroses, but please leave them to seed and multiply so that we can again see the glory of massed primroses in this forest, just as the bluebells have returned to Apes Grove. The trees in rows near the road are part of the GLC nursery from which trees are taken to plant out on GLC estates. It is now possible to transfer fairly mature trees in this way.

Leaving the forest, we have only four miles to complete the round. Passing through Old Chigwell Row village by Clare Hall, we pass by the new reservoir with views over the valley to Chigwell church and distant views over London. Along the road to the left at Chigwell is the old many-gabled Kings Head, made famous as the Maypole in Dickens' *Barnaby Rudge*. Chigwell is a village with many Dickensian connections, and which he often visited. The route from here should follow through Grange Farm Centre to the Roding Valley Country Park. Unfortunately Epping Forest District Council contest the use of this footpath even though it has been used by walkers for over fifty years. Negotiations continue, and perhaps soon you will be able to end the walk this way.

But today you must divert for a mile by road to reach the country park, then beside the river and over the green back to Loughton where the walk began.

A rural round like this is worth taking at all times of year, but particularly in April and May for the early green of the forest foliage, and the birdsong and spring flowers all the way. Or of course in late October for the forests in autumn colour. The weather is mainly kind, without extremes and more generally fine than wet. Epping Forest can be boggy in winter, and the going can be hard over the ploughed fields around White Roding and Theydon Mount from November to March. But by April the fields are usually harrowed and the paths become re-established. Soon too, the route should be waymarked and already many of the paths are indicated at their start by signposts.

Although the Three Forests Way can be walked as a continuous round, it can also very easily be tackled in sections using public transport out and back. One suggestion for a four day walk would begin with the 15 miles from Loughton to Harlow, using the 702 Green Line

Roydon

coach to both points. A second day of 15 miles from Harlow round to Hatfield Broad Oak would use the Eastern National service 58 to return to Bishops Stortford. Check bus times first though. The next section to Ongar would be a $12\frac{1}{2}$ mile walk, ending on the London Transport Central Line, and the last long section of $17\frac{1}{2}$ miles from Ongar back to Loughton is served by Central Line trains at both ends. Other permutations are possible of course, and there are youth hostels at High Beech and Harlow if you prefer to look for overnight accommodation.

The Three Forests Way uses the old-established public footpaths of Essex throughout its length. In this, it serves to give access to the many other hundreds of miles of paths in this beautiful county, and I hope it will make a good start to your further exploration. There are so many walks you could take in Epping Forest for example, that there is a separate booklet available to describe twenty of them. Around Hatfield Forest too, the Bishops Stortford Footpath Society produces a little book with more walks. Yet another book describes twenty short rounds all starting from good parking spots near the Three Forests Way. So try this walk first perhaps as an introduction to the variety and character of the Essex countryside, then explore deeper still.

The Three Forests Way

Progressive Mileage	Miles Between	Places on route	Bus Service to	Rail Service	Cafes	Accommodation	Inns providing snacks etc	Shops	Camping
-	-	Loughton	Bishops Stortford and local services	•	•		•	•	
8	8	Epping Green	Epping		•		•		
13½	5½	Roydon	Local services	•				•	Roydon Mill
16	2½	Harlow	Bishops Stortford, Loughton, Romford, Ongar	•	•		•	•	Caravan Park
20	4	Sawbridgeworth	As above	•	•	•	•	•	
27½	7½	Bishops Stortford (by bus from Takeley at north end of Hatfield Forest)	Takeley (infrequent)	•	•	•	•	•	
31	3½	Hatfield Broad Oak	Bishops Stortford				•	•	
34	3	White Roding	As above				•	•	
43½	9½	Ongar	Harlow	•	•		•	•	
52½	9	Abridge	Romford, Harlow, Bishops Stortford, Theydon Bois, Epping		•		•	•	
57¼	4¾	Chigwell Row	Harlow, Bishops Stortford, Hainault				•	•	
59¼	2	Chigwell	Loughton	•				•	

There are youth hostels at High Beech (Epping Forest) and Harlow

For details of accommodation in the Epping Forest District area, a list is available from the District Council Offices, 323 High Street, Epping, Essex

Early closing: Wednesday afternoon in Roydon, Harlow, Bishops Stortford, Ongar and Abridge, and Thursday in Loughton, Sawbridgeworth, and Chigwell

Essex County Council publish a series of comprehensive bus timetables including all operators. Most of the Three Forests Way is covered by the Epping, Harlow and Loughton section, while a small part is covered by the Bishops Stortford section. They are available from local bus offices in Bishops Stortford, Harlow, etc.

The Viking Way

Brett Collier

If you explore Lincolnshire today, you will meet many reminders of an early page of history in the large number of place names that owe their origins to the Vikings. 'By' in Danish means a village or settlement, and within the old county boundary there are more than 220 names with this ending. Claxby comes from 'klakkr' meaning clod, Orby from 'orre' meaning moorhen, Walesby from 'valr' or falcon, while a Viking, one 'Slengr the Idler' gave his name to Slingsby. In 877 a great Danish army, the Host, seized the part of Mercia that became the area of the Five Boroughs—Lincoln, Stamford, Leicester, Nottingham and Derby. A treaty between Guthrum and Alfred established the Danelaw that covered virtually the whole of eastern England from Tweed to Thames, and for forty years it remained an independent area. By 919, however, Alfred and his successors had reconquered all of Mercia, but the Scandinavian influence continued, for they were left in possession of their land, and retained their customs and laws.

With these many reminders along the route, it was a happy inspiration of Christopher Hall, then secretary of the Ramblers' Association, that gave the name Viking Way to the walk being planned to cross Lincolnshire. Ramblers of RA Lincolnshire Area were devising their route simply to link existing rights of way, but although some of the tracks were very ancient, in no sense was this a route actually followed by the Viking invaders. It was planned very much for today's walkers.

Clearly a county path should come to the county town, so having crossed the wolds from the tidal waters of the Humber, it turns to Lincoln. Our recommended route takes the Viking Way past the cathedral and the castle, appropriately, for Viking remains have been found only recently on an archaeological dig within yards of the castle wall. South of Lincoln, the route makes logical use of the ancient

Sewstern Lane, a neolithic track that existed long before the Vikings, taking the walker to Oakham, once the proud county town of our smallest shire. Although it does not offer wild countryside or the grand dimension it is nevertheless a route of fair contrasts, from the wide horizons of the wolds escarpment, the sweeping valley of the Bain, wooded heathlands around Woodhall Spa, the lonely ruin of Barlings Abbey, the incomparable cathedral on the hill at Lincoln, then the stone-built villages along the cliff southwards, to the gentle wooded hills and fertile valleys of Rutland.

Since that original concept, county boundaries have been reorganised and the first 15 miles of the Viking Way are now in South Humberside, while the final 15 miles have been absorbed into Leicestershire. Perhaps the Way was fortunate in having an influential champion in the late John Hedley-Lewis, a farmer and keen walker, and active president of RA Lincolnshire Area. After the redrawing of boundaries, he became chairman of Lincolnshire County Council and it was largely through his efforts that the Viking Way came into being without further delay. Ramblers have erected a fine oak ladder stile on the Way at Stenwith Bridge, by which to remember him.

In Lincolnshire and South Humberside you will find the route signposted and waymarked with a horned Viking helmet symbol. In Leicestershire too, the waymarking should now be complete, using a variation of Viking helmet over a shield. Alas, both signs and waymarks are continually removed, and Lincolnshire has a volunteer wardening scheme to patrol their section and keep it in good order. Welcome though it is, the waymark actually perpetuates a common myth about our sea raider ancestors. They did not, it seems, wear horned helmets, for in battle these cumbersome devices would only have helped opponents to cleave their skulls. Such helmets may have been worn ceremonially, and have thus been found in burial remains.

From Humber to Lincoln

The Viking Way begins at the Humber Bridge which, when completed, will have the longest main span of any suspension bridge in the world—4626ft. It will have a footway at each side which will link the

Viking Way to the Wolds Way, a path planned to run from North
Ferriby to the cliffs of Filey Brigg. Here it meets the start of the Cleveland Way, so that the three long-distance routes together will offer a
remarkable 300 mile walk. The bridge is just to the west of Barton-
upon-Humber, at one time the most important port on the Humber
and possessing one of the finest Saxon towers in the land. Today it is a
sleepy little market town a mile from the waterside, for Hull across the
estuary has taken away Barton's cargoes and old importance.

Past the old rope walk, the Viking Way runs westwards along the
Humber floodbank by riverside tracks from which there are fine views.
At high tide many cargo ships can be seen plying to and from the port
of Goole and other riverside wharves on the Ouse and Trent. At South
Ferriby, with its tree-clad slopes clinging to the western edge of the
Lincolnshire Wolds, the Way ascends to the top of the escarpment
past a quarry and on to a wide green lane offering fine views over the
Ancholme valley and the flat Read's Island with its single farmhouse and
one tree. Then by field paths to the Burnham–Melton Ross road.
Burnham is one of the numerous places claimed as the site of the famous
battle of Brunanburgh fought in 937 and celebrated in verse in the
Anglo-Saxon Chronicle, where Aethelstan utterly routed Olaf the
Dane.

The Way turns southwards to follow quiet lanes, gradually descending into Barnetby-le-Wold. The village lies at the western end of a
natural gap in the wolds, and three railway lines join here before going
on to the coast. On the A18, just west of the village, can be found
Melton Gallows, erected on the enactment of James I following a visit
to Lincolnshire. Two local families, the Tyrwhits and the Ross's, had a
feud during a hunting expedition in which several had been slain.
James heard of the feud and ordered that if any person was slain in a
further encounter, the perpetrator should be judged a murderer and
hanged. The gallows were erected on the site of the feud, and are
always kept in good condition.

Turning southwards along a farm track, the route comes to the
county boundary and the small village of Bigby, in a charming setting
on the western slope of the wolds with lovely views over the Ancholme
valley. The church has an array of monuments and brasses, some of

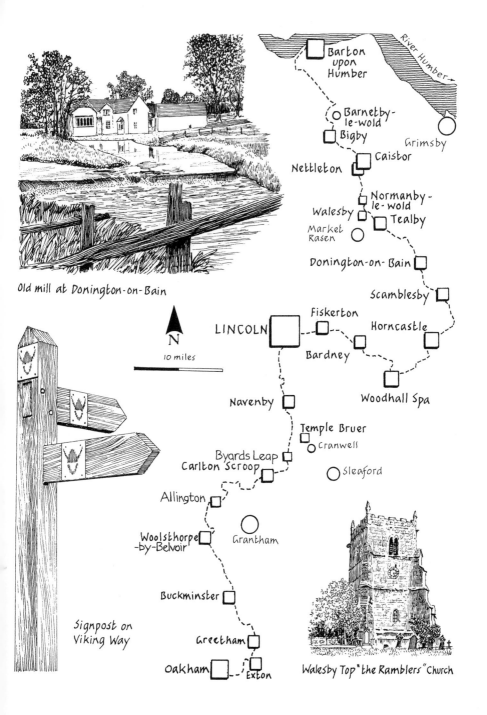

Old mill at Donington-on-Bain

River Humber

Barton upon Humber

Barnetby-le-wold

Bigby

Grimsby

Caistor

Nettleton

Normanby-le-wold

Walesby

Tealby

Market Rasen

Donington-on-Bain

Scamblesby

Fiskerton

LINCOLN

Horncastle

N

10 miles

Bardney

Woodhall Spa

Navenby

Temple Bruer

Cranwell

Byards Leap

Carlton Scroop

Sleaford

Allington

Woolsthorpe-by-Belvoir

Grantham

Buckminster

Signpost on Viking Way

Greetham

Oakham

Exton

Walesby Top "the Ramblers" Church

them to the Tyrwhits who lived nearby. Kneeling in the sanctuary are Sir Robert Tyrwhit and his wife, Lady Bridget Manners, now headless. She was a Maid of Honour to Elizabeth I, and made a runaway marriage with her husband. Round a Tyrwhit altar tomb are the words of the 128th Psalm and the figures of their twenty-two children, little bundles representing those that died at birth.

The first Lincolnshire section of the Way traverses part of the west escarpment of the Lincolnshire Wolds and includes the county top at 550ft, and some of the highest land in eastern England. Through a succession of spring-line villages—Bigby, Somerby, Searby, Owmby, Grasby and Clixby—we come to Caistor, an attractive little place developed around a Roman walled town that may have had its origin through a spring with health giving properties—a Roman spa. Parts of the Roman wall may still be seen near the church. In these villages, the pattern created by early settlements has persisted until this day. They were established along the edges of both the limestone and the chalk uplands because of the need of early inhabitants for food, water and possibly defence. Here the porous rocks give way to the heavier underlying clays and hence there are many springs. The location also enabled the inhabitants to use both the heath above and the meadows below which they needed for their cattle.

A short journey down the scarp leads us to Nettleton, where the Way now enters that part of the wolds designated as an Area of Outstanding Natural Beauty. The path ascends again to the wold top past Normanby-le-Wold, the county's highest hamlet where the Jubilee Beacon was lit in 1977. Across the valley on the opposite hillside can be seen Walesby Top old church, the restored ironstone-built church of All Saints, widely known as 'the ramblers' church'. It has a stained glass window depicting ramblers and cyclists passing through a cornfield, and each Trinity Sunday a well attended ramblers' service is held in the ancient church.

Over the hilltop past the church, the Way continues up and down a very steep valley and on to the lovely village of Tealby under a steep slope of the wolds. The village and its church have Tennyson connections, for members of the family lived at Bayons Manor nearby. The manor belonged to William the Conqueror's half brother Odo, Bishop

Walesby Top old church, the 'ramblers' church' on the Viking Way
(*Lincolnshire Echo*)

of Bayeaux, and the name Bayons is a direct link with him. Tennyson's
uncle made Bayons Manor into a stately battlemented house complete
with drawbridge and barbican, but unfortunately it was destroyed in
1964. Our route passes the site of the manor and up the slope to cross
High Street, an ancient ridge-top track connecting Horncastle to
Caistor. The two united villages of Ludford Parva and Ludford Magna
are on the line of the so-called Salters Way, a prehistoric route that ran
from the coastal plain over the heathlands to Salterford and Saltby, and
on into the Midlands.

At the head of the valley of the river Bain (a Danish river name) are
several village sites, Grimblethorpe, Calcethorpe, West Wykeham,
South Cadeby and Girsby, that have either shrunk to hamlets or perhaps
a single farm. For a century or so after the Black Death of 1349, these
villages gradually declined because of the changing pattern of trade,
the quality of the soil and the fact that they never fully recovered from
the devastation.

Donington-on-Bain, Scamblesby, Belchford and Fulletby bring us
to Horncastle, a pleasant little town where the wolds come down to the
fens. It was a walled town in Roman times, and played a part in the
Civil War. A Roman station was established here, Banovallum, 'the
next station after Lincoln', and was made defensible by a vallum
crossing the peninsular point of land shaped like a horn—thus Hyrn-
ceaster. Portions of the Roman wall still exist behind some of the
buildings.

The Way leaves Horncastle by the south bank of the canal and
continues for 7 miles along the Spa Trail, a disused railway line to
Woodhall Spa. The town was described in an old guide book as 'a
place rapidly rising in importance for the cure of gout and rheumatism
and scrofulous diseases', although it was scarcely known outside the
county at that time. The spa was accidentally discovered in an un-
successful attempt at boring for coal, and it was stated that the amount
of iodine and bromine in the water far exceeded that of any other spa in
England. The next section of the route between Woodhall Spa and
Lincoln follows the valley of the River Witham, and the sandy soil of
Woodhall with its gorse, heather, pine and birches gives way to the
peat and alluvium which characterises the flood plain of the Witham.
Here we are on the edge of the fen, and an intricate system of delphs
make possible the intense cultivation of these rich peat soils.

For many miles around, the British Sugar Corporation's beet factory
at Bardney is a prominent landmark, throwing up plumes of white
smoke for several months each year when it is at full capacity. Stixwould and Southrey with its little 'home-made' wooden church, bring
us to Bardney, a village that grew up around the great Benedictine
Abbey, one of the most famous and oldest in England. The whole of
this district along the Witham was thickly set with monastic houses.
Bardney, Barlings, Tupholme, Stainfield and Stixwould were within a
few miles. Bardney Abbey was founded in 607—an island stronghold
surrounded by waters of the fen and guarded on all sides by great
forests. Etheldred, King of Mercia, resigned his crown in 705 to
become a monk and eventually its abbot after his predecessor had been
murdered by the Danes. The abbey was again pillaged and burnt in
870, when the Danes put some 300 monks and lay brethren to the

sword during the terrible invasion of Hinguar and Hubba. For two centuries the abbey was in ruins until rebuilt by William de Gaunt, Earl of Lincoln, as a Benedictine foundation. At the Dissolution, no district suffered more, and only the merest fragments remain of any of these five houses.

Leaving Bardney by the bridge over the Witham, the present route of the Viking Way follows the west bank of the river for a short distance and then the south bank of the South Delph for nine long, straight, windswept miles that end in Lincoln at a factory car park. This was not the route recommended by the Ramblers' Association, and the local group can provide a route guide for a longer but pleasanter way into the city.

This recommended alternative takes us out of Bardney on the Wragby road, then across a little-used footpath that passes by a tumulus known locally as King's Hill Close, believed to be the burial place of Ethelred, the king who became Abbot of Bardney. The route then follows Forestry Commission woods and across open fields to Stainfield, held for centuries by the Tyrwhit family, mentioned earlier in the grim context of Melton Gallows. A bridleway across lonely fields brings us to the one remaining inner wall of Barlings Abbey still standing. The ruin can be seen from a distance, for it stands on a slight rise above the Barlings Eau. The Abbot of Barlings, under the name of Captain Cobbler, led the Lincolnshire rebels in the reign of Henry VIII and was later executed at Tyburn along with the Vicar of Louth.

At Fiskerton (in Scandinavian 'the fishermen's village'), we follow the north bank of the river Witham until the little church of Greetwell is reached. This tiny place is said to derive its name from a spring which runs into the river below. It was mentioned in Domesday, but today it is but a single farm. Now, 2 miles of field path with wide views across the Witham valley to Washingborough and beyond, lead to Lincoln, described many years ago as 'this old confused town—long, uneven, steep and rugged'. Lincoln is derived from the Lindum Colonia of the Romans, but they only adapted the earlier name of Lindon belonging to the Celtic settlement. Lin means a pool or lake, and dun or don a hill-fort, so that Lindon meant a hill-fort by the pool. The city has played a part in England's story for over 2,000 years for there was a

Lincoln Castle, on the ramblers' recommended route for the Viking Way (*Lincolnshire Echo*)

Celtic settlement on the hilltop long before Julius Caesar landed on our shores. Celts, Romans, Saxons, Danes and Normans all came in their turn and made a contribution to the city.

Our recommended route brings us into the city by Greetwellgate to Eastgate where the cathedral, seen in the distance for so many miles along the Way, may be viewed at last in all its glory, rising from the lawns of Minster Green. There stands the statue of that English poet who belongs so specially to Lincolnshire, Alfred Lord Tennyson with his beloved wolfhound Karenina beside him.

It was in 1072 that William the Conqueror gave a charter to Bishop Remigius for the building of a cathedral in Lincoln and the building was completed twenty years later. However in 1141 it was destroyed by fire, and an earthquake in 1185 meant that the structure had again to be rebuilt. The task was undertaken by St Hugh of Avalon who completed the third largest English cathedral, in Lincolnshire oolite in 1200. Through the cloisters you can visit the chapter house where the story of the cathedral is told in stained glass from the Conqueror's charter up to the last visit of John Wesley in 1790. Cross under Exchequergate Arch to Castle Square and its splendid castle which William I erected in 1068. The imposing eastern gateway of the castle is fourteenth century but it does contain Norman tunnel vaulting.

Lincoln to Oakham

Leaving uphill by the aptly named Steep Hill with its ancient buildings, cafes, bookshops and antique dealers, we descend to the High Street and proceed through the Stonebow as far as the High Bridge, the only bridge now remaining in England that preserves the shops on it. From the bridge we follow the Witham bank footway to Thorn Bridge to rejoin the Viking Way, leaving the busy road at South Common to climb once more to the edge of the escarpment with extensive views towards the Trent and Nottinghamshire. The path takes us through half a dozen attractive stone-built villages along the cliff before turning across Welbourn Heath, proceeding for several miles along the green lane known as High Dyke, up to 120ft wide in places, the Roman Ermine Street.

Steep Hill, Lincoln

Eastward from Welbourn but a mile away at Temple Bruer may be seen a 54ft high tower rising above grey farm buildings which, in the thirteenth century, was the south chancel tower of the round church of the Holy Sepulchre, restored in 1961. It is the remnant of one of Lincolnshire's five preceptories of the Order of Knights Templars, whose houses were linked in a chain extending throughout Europe.

Following High Dyke past Cocked Hat Plantation, the next landmark eastwards is the impressive dome of the Royal Air Force College at Cranwell high above the trees. The magnificent college buildings were built in 1933 to designs by Sir James Grey-West in the style of Chelsea Hospital.

Where High Dyke meets the A17 Sleaford–Newark road at Byard's Leap, look in the long grass of the verge of the lay-by. Enormous horseshoes mark the distance of the leap of the blind horse Byard when the old witch attacked him and his rider Black Jim. You can read the legend in a glass case on the outside wall of the cafe.

Ermine Street now becomes the metalled B6403 going dead straight for 4 miles along the windswept 'agger' to Ancaster village, the small Roman town of Causennae. The Viking Way follows the wide road verge for the first 2 miles before turning westwards to Carlton Scroop. Here the Viking Way leaves the cliff ridge to descend into the valley of the Witham. This remarkable oolite escarpment known as 'The Cliff' is the steep western face of the long wold range extending continuously from Leicestershire to the Humber, broken only by the gorge of the Witham at Lincoln. The number of fine churches in these villages is no doubt largely due to the abundance and excellence of the building stone from Ancaster quarries. This limestone is noted for its special quality of hardening soon after exposure.

The Viking Way continues southwards to skirt the homely village of Foston and, after crossing the Great North Road, takes a pleasant farm track to the secluded village of Allington, close by the Leicestershire border. Now we follow Sewstern Lane, a route that is so ancient that its origins are unknown but it was certainly in use during the Iron Age. This drift road was used throughout the Middle Ages as a route between the great fairs of Nottingham and Stamford, and later to connect the court at Belvoir Castle to the Royal Court in London. With the advent of public coaches and turnpike roads in the seventeenth century, the old way fell out of use as it passed through no town or village with accommodation for nearly thirty miles.

On the lane at Stenwith Bridge near Woolsthorpe, you will be climbing over a fine oak ladder stile and reading on its side the dedication to John Hedley-Lewis who sadly was too ill to attend the Viking Way inauguration ceremony and died shortly afterwards.

Now the way follows the tow-path of the disused Grantham Canal for a short distance before rejoining Sewster Lane at Brewer's Grave. This is reputedly the unconsecrated grave of a brewer employed at Belvoir Castle who, in a fit of drunkenness, drowned himself in a vat of ale. Where the lane crosses the road is the start of a splendid waymarked $17\frac{1}{2}$ mile route to Melton Mowbray called the Jubilee Way.

Although hills and trees intervene from time to time along Sewstern Lane, there are many fine views of Belvoir Castle standing on its spur of the wolds. It takes its name from the French word belle voir, meaning a fine site or view and one can appreciate and endorse the description of 'Lordly Belvoir' for it is strongly reminiscent of Windsor Castle. From the Vale of Belvoir and the flat lands beyond, from the cliff spurs south of Lincoln and even from Lincoln cathedral itself, a full 30 miles away, it is possible to see the castle on a good day. It was an important Royalist centre during the Civil War, destroyed by order of Parliament but rebuilt in 1668 and again in 1801.

The next few miles after Brewer's Grave are perhaps the most exciting and beautiful section of the lane. The village of Denton, set in a hollow near the Leicestershire border, has well-built cottages with warm brown stone walls and mellow red roofs. There is a great house in the park and a spring called St Christopher's Well filling a group of lakes. The church stands in a lovely position overlooking one of the lakes in the park.

The disused airfield at Saltby Heath will become a mine tip if the Vale of Belvoir coalfield plans gain government approval. Just north of today's airfield site, King Lud of Mercia built defensive earthworks against attack from the lane. As well as our own ancient way on the north–south line, Saltby is on another prehistoric route that ran from the saltpans of the coastal plain, across the heathland and to the Midlands. It is also believed to have been the burial ground of some forgotten chief and beyond doubt this secluded spot is of very great antiquity. Yet this area is also the proposed site for a mine shaft with winding gear tower as high as a 22-storey office block.

At Buckminster the Saxon Bucca built a minster but there is no trace today—the church may occupy the site. It is a pleasant place standing high up in the wolds with a dignified Georgian hall and park. Cribbs Lodge gains its name from a fight held in 1811 between Tom Cribb, champion of England and a negro, Tom Molyneux. Such a fight at that time was illegal, and it was held at a point where the three counties of Leicestershire, Rutland and Lincolnshire met so that a quick escape could be made over a border to avoid the local magistrate. Watched by 15,000 people, Cribb won after twenty minutes.

Exton is a truly delightful English village with its pub on the green appropriately called the Fox and Hounds, and houses of Rutland limestone and Colly Weston slates; the old church situated in the park is one of the finest in the country and contains a superb collection of tombs and monuments, well worth a detour. From Exton we follow the mile-long Barnsdale Avenue with its splendid beeches, sycamores, ash, chestnuts and birches to descend to the western end of Rutland Water by Burley Wood.

The banqueting hall of Oakham Castle at the end of the Viking Way, with its remarkable collection of horseshoes gathered by tradition from every peer passing through the town (*Leonard and Marjorie Gayton*)

The famous house at Burley on the Hill is a magnificent building with a Doric colonnade extending nearly 200ft along the north front. Battered down by the Parliamentarian army during the Civil War, it has been rebuilt and burnt down and rebuilt again.

The whole of this undulating wolds landscape is ideal fox-hunting country and the Belvoir and Cottesmore packs are two of the best known in England. During the last century, great landowners planted small woods or coverts for foxes to breed and live in. These coverts, now matured, blend in well with the countryside, many of them covering up to 100 acres.

We meet the A606 at the western end of Rutland Water, the largest man-made lake in Europe. To the west, 2 miles away, the lovely spire of All Saints, Oakham's parish church, can be seen rising above the Vale of Catmose. Its famous weathervane, Cock Peter, leads us to the end of the Viking Way in this compact little market town. It has a well-preserved market place with a set of stocks (strangely with five holes), a butter cross and the original sixteenth-century buildings of Oakham School. Through an old gateway along a little lane just off the market square is the twelfth-century banqueting hall of a manor house long known as Oakham Castle. The castle belonged to the Earl of Ferrers, whose name means ferrier or blacksmith, and is said to be descended from William the Conqueror's blacksmith. It has been one of the quaint customs of the town to collect a horseshoe from every peer of the realm who passes through and there is a remarkable collection of all sizes of horseshoe, some over three feet high, many with crowns and all with the names of donors. Just across the main street is a fine new museum well worth a visit at the end of your journey through history from the Humber bank to Rutland Water.

The Viking Way

Progressive Mileage	Miles Between	Places on route	Bus service to	Rail Service	Cafes	Accommodation	Inns providing snacks etc	Shops	Camping
–	–	Barton-upon Humber	Lincoln, Brigg, Grimsby	●	●	●	●	●	
13	13	Barnetby-le-Wold	Brigg, Scunthorpe Grimsby	●	●	●	●	●	
18	5	Caistor	Grimsby, Market Rasen		●	●	●	●	
27	9	Tealby	Lincoln, Grimsby		●		●	●	
*		Market Rasen	Lincoln, Grimsby	●	●	●	●	●	
37	10	Donington on Bain	Market Stainton, Louth			●	●	●	
42	5	Scamblesby	Louth, Horncastle			●	●	●	●
55	13	Horncastle	Lincoln, Bardney, Skegness		●	●	●	●	
61	6	Woodhall Spa	Boston, Lincoln		●	●	●	●	●
68	7	Bardney	Lincoln, Horncastle		●	●	●	●	
80	12	Lincoln	Grantham, Grimsby	●	●	●	●	●	
90	10	Navenby	Lincoln, Grantham			●	●	●	
96½	6½	Byard's Leap	Sleaford, Newark		●¹	●			
100½	4	Carlton Scroop	Lincoln, Grantham						
106	5½	Marston	Grantham			●	●	●	●
*		Grantham	Woolsthorpe, Buckminster, Melton Mowbray	●	●	●	●	●	
117	11	Woolsthorpe-by-Belvoir	Grantham, Eaton			●	●	●	
124	7½	Buckminster	Grantham, Melton Mowbray			●	●	●	
132	8	Greetham	Stamford, Oakham Grantham			●	●	●	
135	3	Exton	Oakham, Stamford			●	●	●	
140	5	Oakham	Grantham, Greetham	●	●	●	●	●	

* Not actually on the Way   ¹Summer only

There are youth hostels at Lincoln and Grantham

Early closing: Wednesday afternoon at Caistor, Horncastle, Woodhall Spa, Bardney, Lincoln and Grantham. Thursday afternoon at Barton, Market Rasen and Oakham

The Oxfordshire Way

Alison Kemp

The Oxfordshire Way is a quiet walk through quiet farming country. It was originally conceived by the Rights of Way Committee of the Oxfordshire Branch of the Council for the Protection of Rural England (CPRE), to link the Cotswolds and the Chilterns. The first line for the route was roughed out by enthusiasts round a dining table in a candlelit room. Happily it was the idea and not the maps which caught fire. That was about eight years ago, so it seems that the prophecy will be fulfilled that it would take ten years to turn a long-distance path from a line on a map into a first-class route on the ground.

It was at once decided that only existing public rights of way should be used, as the prospect of persuading landowners and the county council to negotiate the creation of new footpaths was too daunting. This proved a wise decision, as our Rights of Way Committee was able to set to work straight away to survey and modify the original route. In this task CPRE had the invaluable help of several members of the Oxfordshire Fieldpaths Society and the Chiltern Society. Later on they were joined by the Ramblers' Association which set up its first group in Oxfordshire in 1973.

It took about three years to complete the first survey, to compile a schedule of all the defects encountered, and finally to transfer the route on to special maps. This was an extremely difficult task, as it involved working with thirteen sheets of the county definitive map that recorded all the rights of way, but CPRE was lucky to have a talented cartographer who tackled the problems with great skill. By 1976 it was possible to bring the whole idea of the Oxfordshire Way to the attention of the county council.

The council was immediately interested, and allocated the sum of £2,000 to be spent on the route. One of the first tasks was to signpost

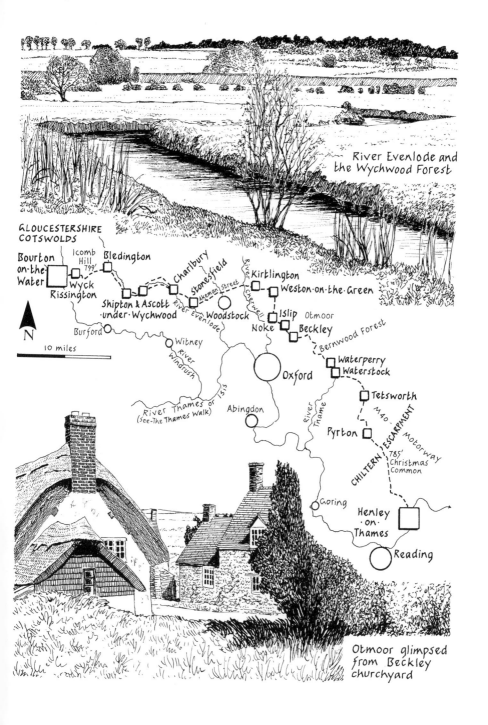

River Evenlode and the Wychwood Forest

GLOUCESTERSHIRE COTSWOLDS

Bourton on-the-Water

Icomb Hill 799'

Bledington

Wyck Rissington

Shipton & Ascott under-Wychwood

Charlbury

Stonesfield

Akeman Street

Woodstock

River Evenlode

Kirtlington

Weston-on-the-Green

River Cherwell

Islip

Noke

Otmoor

Beckley

Bernwood Forest

N

10 miles

Burford

Witney

River Windrush

Oxford

River Thames or Isis (see-The Thames Walk)

Abingdon

Waterperry

Waterstock

Tetsworth

River Thame

Pyrton

M40 Motorway

CHILTERN ESCARPMENT

785' Christmas Common

Goring

Henley on Thames

Reading

Otmoor glimpsed from Beckley churchyard

it. Special signs were designed and the signposting, wherever the route touched the metalled roads, was completed by the beginning of 1978. The county council also installed and repaired footbridges where necessary, and cleared heavy undergrowth which would have defied the efforts of voluntary workers with handtools. There still remained, however, a good deal of maintenance and repair work to be done, so the council applied to the Countryside Commission for a grant, and was promised fifty per cent of its expenditure on the Oxfordshire Way for the following three years. Work under this financial provision is now going ahead, over £4,000 having already been spent since 1976. The county council also undertook to consult all land occupiers on the route over waymarking, and produced a special waymark for the use of the voluntary societies. The Gloucestershire County Council was equally helpful over the ten miles at the western end that lie in the designated Cotswold Area of Outstanding Natural Beauty, and is mainly in Gloucestershire. Their chief warden with his voluntary helpers did all the waymarking there, not quibbling over the fact that the word Oxfordshire appeared within their own county boundary.

Meantime CPRE had begun to publicise the Oxfordshire Way, through its own branch activities and through the local press and Radio Oxford, both of which gave splendid coverage to the project. Quite a number of people seemed interested, and the first printing of 2,000 maps was exhausted by the end of 1978. In that year CPRE produced its own guide, and this too had to be reprinted within the year.

The Oxfordshire Way has never been officially opened; it has simply become better known and better used with every passing month. An official opening might in any case be somewhat inappropriate, since the route is composed entirely of existing rights of way. Most of its component paths have been in daily use for centuries, and the only thing new about the Oxfordshire Way is that it draws attention to the fact that even today one can walk from Bourton-on-the-Water to Henley-upon-Thames along the ancient tracks and highways of the county.

Oxfordshire is not a county of dramatic landscapes. It has no mountains, moors or great lakes. It is a county of rich farmlands, gentle river

The waymarked Way above the Evenlode, heading towards Charlbury
(*David Sharp*)

valleys, noble parks, and, above all, enchanting villages that have
preserved, even in the twentieth century, their vernacular style. Most
of the houses are of limestone, with stone-tiled roofs, until one comes to
the flint walls and clay tiles of the Chilterns. Many of the Cotswold
trees, alas, were elms, but Chiltern beeches and riverside willows as well
as fragments of ancient forests at Charlbury and Waterperry still give
the county a reasonably well-wooded appearance.

The Oxfordshire Way is only 65 miles long, yet it takes the traveller
through a remarkably varied landscape. From Bourton-on-the-Water
he will pass through Cotswold limestone, the Oxford clay vale, the
Oxford Corallian Heights, the gault clay vale, and finally, the Chiltern
chalk. The route climbs to over 800ft at Wyck Beacon, then drops

down into the Windrush valley and over into the Evenlode valley with its lovely little stone villages and its glimpses of the last remnants of the old forest of Wychwood. Soon after Charlbury on the Evenlode it joins Akeman Street, and on this historic Roman road sweeps straight through the splendours of Blenheim Park and on towards yet a third lovely river valley, the Cherwell. Soon the whole landscape changes, and the walker suddenly finds himself looking down into the mysterious chequered marshland of Otmoor. After this one begins to lose the Cotswold villages, snug behind their stone walls, for the stone gives way to brick and then flint, the stone-tiled roofs to thatch or clay tiles, as the Way approaches the Chiltern escarpment. The Chilterns are a total contrast to the Cotswolds, though Christmas Common near the end of the Way, is only a few feet lower than Wyck Beacon at the beginning.

It is this ever-changing landscape that makes the Oxfordshire Way such a delight to walk. Every kind of lowland wild flower can be found somewhere along the way, and it passes straight through two nature reserves, managed by the Berkshire, Buckinghamshire and Oxfordshire Naturalists Trust. The first is at Bruern, a few miles from the beginning of the Way, the second at Swyncombe, only a short distance from Henley. Within a single day's walking you can be pottering beside a gentle little river, or standing on a windy upland where the skies are huge and the views exhilarating, so that naturally the fauna is as varied as the flora. The walker will be unlucky if he fails to catch a glimpse of a heron or a kingfisher in one of the river valleys, or to enjoy a clutch of mallard ducklings or dabchicks essaying their first swim. He may meet a fox, most likely a deer, and hares and rabbits, watervoles, shrews, weasels and innumerable little creatures will bear him company from time to time. For the Oxfordshire Way is, above all else, an extended country walk along hedgerows and streams, up grassy slopes and by the edge of pastures and cornfields.

It is not a long-distance path to be tackled with too much vigour and determination as to mileage to be covered each day. There is so much to see and enjoy along its length, so many attractive corners beckoning one to sit and rest awhile. Best of all, there are the villages along the route or easily reached by small detours for those in search of shop, pub or post office. Nearly all Oxfordshire villages are beautiful. It seems that our forebears who built in stone and flint had an instinctive understanding of the harmony that such materials have with the countryside, out of which the houses seem almost to grow. The stone villages, their walls effortlessly clothed with aubretia in spring, valerian and roses in summer, seem to group themselves comfortably together for company. The flint houses of the Chilterns, often around trim village greens, seem equally companionable. Nearly all the parish churches are worth a visit, Bledington for instance with its magnificent stonework, little Shorthampton with its wall paintings and box pews, Islip with its connections with Edward the Confessor who was born there in 1004. In Noke the church is much smaller than the rectory, Waterperry has a Saxon arch, a wooden tower and some outstanding brasses. Perhaps the most interesting church of all is Rycote Chapel, beautifully restored by the Department of the Environment and containing a splendidly pretentious royal pew installed for the use of Queen Elizabeth I. The grandeur of this erection is only rivalled by the adjacent family pew, which outclasses its royal neighbour by having two stories.

There is plenty of our past still visible along the walk. At its very start, less than a mile out of Bourton-on-the-Water, the Oxfordshire Way is guarded by the Iron Age hill fort called Salmondsbury Camp. Wyck Beacon, highest point on the route, is a 6ft high round barrow on top of the hill. At many places along the way, the discerning eye can pick out traces of the earthworks of our ancestors, and for the best part of 5 miles the walker follows Akeman Street, treading the same good road that echoed to the feet of the marching Roman legions. Today the road is clearly visible even across the fields, a raised way with one substantial bank that has served as a parish boundary over the centuries. By a small detour via the delectable Stonesfield Ford and its footbridge over the Evenlode, you can visit a well-excavated Roman villa at East End, North Leigh. At Pyrton the route crosses the Icknield Way, a much older track than even Akeman Street, where you might meet walkers following the long-distance Ridgeway Path.

Most of the villages on the Oxfordshire Way are named in the Domesday Book and some, like the deserted villages of Whitehill and Stoke Talmage, now lie silent beneath the turf, only to be detected by humps and depressions in the surrounding fields. At Islip, Oliver Cromwell defeated royalist troops in a brisk skirmish; on Otmoor the inhabitants of the Seven Towns fought desperately against the enclosure of their swampy pastures, so that the Otmoor Riots of 1830 are still remembered. They did not, alas, save the moor from 'progress' and today there are new threats to this ecologically precious wetland. Modern drainage and hedge removal are altering its character yearly, and in a few years motorists speeding across Otmoor on the great new road that threatens to carve it in two will probably wonder why there was so much anguish at the loss of this once lonely, wild, bird-filled place.

The eighteenth century is much in evidence all along the Oxfordshire Way. Probably most of the village houses were built then, though many delightful seventeenth-century cottages keep them company.

The Cotswold stone farm houses of Wyck Rissington (*David Sharp*)

Many of the fields, neat rectangles with hawthorn hedges, and the straight walled or hedged roads with their wide verges are evidence of the extent to which the parliamentary enclosures of the late eighteenth and early nineteenth centuries altered the Oxfordshire landscape. But although they altered it, and neat Georgian farmhouses are dotted about the enclosed countryside, much of the old farming pattern survived. In many a pasture the ridge and furrow of the old open fields can still be seen and many of the present hedges are centuries older than the neat hawthorn and ash of the parliamentary enclosures. Small odd-shaped fields with splendidly varied hedgerows, and bridleroads running between hedges that have been growing for seven hundred years or more are visual reminders of the medieval way of life that still leaves its imprint on the twentieth-century landscape. On many of the paths that go to make up the Oxfordshire Way, the walker of today is treading in the footsteps of generations of his forebears.

The greatest of all great houses is undoubtedly Blenheim Palace, and its park is worthy of the grandeur of the house. But more to some peoples' taste might be the remote deep-red brick simplicity of Beckley Park, a house which can trace its history back to King Alfred's day when perhaps the triple moats were dug, though the present house was not built until about 1540 by that redoubtable Oxfordshire house-builder, Lord Williams of Thame. He also built Weston Manor, now a hotel, at Weston-on-the-Green. Studley Priory, also now a hotel, was an Elizabethan stately home completed in 1587. It was chosen to portray Sir Thomas More's house in the film of *A Man for all Seasons*. Shipton Court in Shipton-under-Wychwood is one of the largest early Jacobean houses in the county, being built in 1603. Hordley Farm near Wootton is a delightful mixture of sixteenth- and eighteenth-century architecture. The Shaven Crown at Shipton-under-Wychwood has been a hostelry for over 500 years. Probably a good many of the pubs along the way have been sustaining travellers for almost as long, though many of the old inns have now been converted to private houses. Islip for instance once had twenty-one inns, for it lay on the coaching route from London to Worcester. The coaches no longer rattle triumphantly into Islip, and the road pattern has changed. No one goes to Worcester that way any more, which is just as well when you consider modern traffic and Islip's steep and narrow lanes. So there are only two inns now, and Islip has regained the peace it enjoyed before the coaching days.

There is also something for the industrial archaeologist along the walk. Still visible are many of the old quarries at Stonesfield, from whence came the beautiful stone tiles that are the crowning glory of Cotswold villages and grace the roofs of many an Oxford college. The glove industry at Charlbury, Stonesfield and Wootton can still be traced in house and street names. The river valleys have many and various mills, and for the student of railways there is the grandiose brick warehouse at Shipton-under-Wychwood station and the delicious little pavilion-like structure, said to have been designed by Brunel himself, which serves the many passengers who daily commute from Charlbury.

St. James, Stonesfield

So there is plenty to interest all manner of ramblers, young and old, along the Oxfordshire Way. Indeed one of its great virtues is that it provides so many different kinds of walking. The whole route can be covered comfortably in a long weekend by a fairly determined walker, though the problem of overnight accommodation is none too easy on all stretches. The youth hostel at Stow-on-the-Wold is less than 4 miles from the start of the Way. The next hostel is at Charlbury, 15 miles on. Beckley is only 4 miles from the hostel at Oxford but there is unfortunately no bus service. There is, however, a good bus service to Oxford from Islip, 7 miles away. No other hostels are handy until you pass the one attached to the little Friends Meeting House in Henley at the end of the walk, but in a number of the large villages you can find either a pub or hotel which will provide bed and breakfast or, failing that, a reasonable bus service to a sizeable town.

Those who tackle the Oxfordshire Way at any time of the year will find no really challenging difficulties to be encountered, and it is eminently suitable for family parties, nature lovers, and unambitious strollers through the countryside. To be sure, there are plenty of hills to climb, but none to tax the strength or induce vertigo. This is not to say that conditions are always easy. The public field paths of Oxfordshire were badly neglected during the fifties and sixties, and the state of some of them still leaves much to be desired. Many stiles are rickety, and there is far too much barbed wire slung about some of them. Gates are sometimes extremely difficult to open, and even harder to shut. Most of the footbridges are serviceable, but some are quite primitive. All these defects will be remedied in time through the good offices of the county council, but even finding out who farms the land, and is therefore responsible for barbed wire or a broken stile, can be a formidable task. The same problem has slowed down the waymarking, though over half the route is now dealt with. It has taken the county council over two years to track down all land-occupiers in order to carry out the necessary consultations over waymarking, and there are still two or three short stretches where differences of opinion or recalcitrance on the part of the farmers are causing delays. Once the consultations have been held, the voluntary societies have been able to put up their way-marks in the form of yellow or blue arrows on a white disc with the letters OW superimposed. Similar discs, bearing the words 'Oxford-shire Way', are used for the stout elm signposts that stand wherever the path meets a road.

It takes a long time to persuade some farmers that the public have an absolute right to walk the public field paths over their land, and that they, for their part, have no right at all to ignore their statutory obligations over ploughing up rights of way. So there are sadly still places on the Oxfordshire Way where the path regularly disappears under the plough, with never an attempt at reinstatement of the surface. In some of these cases sensible diversions are being arranged, in others the path is quickly trodden out by human feet, but no one can pretend that walking over heavy, ploughed land or through thigh-high crops is anything but a chore. Perhaps one day all farmers will come to respect their legal obligations, to refrain altogether from ploughing the paths that follow field boundaries, and leave in walkable condition the paths that cross their fields.

Approaching Beckley, the Way gives a fine view over Otmoor (*David Sharp*)

What time of year should you choose to walk the Oxfordshire Way? It will be safe enough at any time, but there is enough low-lying land to make it pretty heavy going in the wet months of the year. The meadows near Bourton-on-the-Water confirm the aptness of that village's name. Otmoor is marshland, and it is sometimes a protracted paddle between Noke and Beckley. In a wet winter the Evenlode often spreads out into its water meadows, and the northern of the two alternative routes between Ascott-under-Wychwood and Charlbury can lie under flood. The odd stretches of ploughland, especially in the Otmoor and Tetsworth areas, can be purgatory after a week's rain, but a great deal of the route is over the uplands and affords reasonable walking at any time of year.

Otherwise, for those using the Way for a day's walking, or simply an extended country stroll, there will be particular delights in any month. April and May are probably best for the Chilterns, to catch the full glory of the bluebells beneath the wonderful spring green of the beeches; or October for the superb autumn colours. Along the river valleys high summer is best, for it is in July and August that the river banks are a tapestry of wild flowers—purple loosestrife, henbane, hemp agrimony, comfrey, willowherb, yellow bedstraw, scabious and a score beside, which provide a fit background to the blue flash of a kingfisher. High summer is best too for the Cotswold roadside verges which are carpeted with yellow bedstraw, the mauve of scabious and meadow cranesbill and the bold purple of knapweed. But spring is probably the best for the route as a whole, for round any corner one might encounter primroses or cowslips starring the meadows, violets or bluebells under the hedges. With the scent of hawthorn in your nostrils, the sound of a lark or cuckoo overhead and the sudden plop of a watervole in the placid little river by your side, you can experience on the Oxfordshire Way the true delight of the English countryside in spring.

Now that it is becoming waymarked and well walked, the Oxfordshire Way offers a good basis for easy outings and afternoon strolls that use a short section of it as an introduction to the countryside around. The possibilities are almost endless and the best plan is to study the appropriate OS 1:50 000 series maps. These will not actually label the Oxfordshire Way, but all rights of way are shown and you will easily identify the ones used for our walk, and the many others that link with it. There are, for example, some lovely bridleways, many of them running between ancient hedges, that join up with the Oxfordshire Way near Charlbury. Also the Roman road that crosses Otmoor from north to south, and another bridleway going east and west, both of which give access to the loneliest part of the moor, though you must be prepared to be barred from using them when the firing range is in use, which is all too often in summer months. Between Christmas Common and Henley there are many ways to turn off and explore the Chilterns via its excellent network of footpaths.

The best rail access is Charlbury station on the Paddington–Worcester line. Nearly all the inter-city trains stop at Charlbury and there is also a local service known as the Cotswold Line, between Evesham and Oxford, which stops at Shipton-under-Wychwood, Ascott-under-Wychwood and Bladon for Blenheim. These local trains are few and far between though. The best bus access is at the point where the Oxfordshire Way crosses the A34 north of Woodstock. Here you can pick up a bus to Oxford, Stratford-on-Avon or Birmingham. For the rest of the route one is relying on local bus services run by City of Oxford Motor Service, whose main station is at Gloucester Green, Oxford. The telephone number for travel information on weekdays is Oxford 44138, or at night and on Sundays Oxford 774611. There is also a useful service for some of the villages in the central portion of the route, run by Worth's Motor Services, Enstone, Oxon, telephone Enstone 322.

The Oxfordshire Way is not for those who want to experience the grandeur of solitary places. It is not that sort of long-distance path at all. It is, like the villages it passes through, a comfortable, domesticated, settled kind of path, rich in history, varied in beauty, manageable in scale. For those who enjoy English countryside where people live harmoniously in a still unspoilt rural setting, the Oxfordshire Way has much to offer. There are still orchids in the meadows near Bourton-on-the-Water, and deer in the woodlands near Henley. Oxfordshire still retains its own character.

The Oxfordshire Way

Progressive Mileage	Miles Between	Places on route	Bus service to	Rail Service	Cafes	Accommodation	Inns providing snacks etc	Shops	Camping
-	-	Bourton-on-the-Water	Cheltenham		•	•	•	•	
6¼	6¼	Bledington	—		•		•	•	
9½	3¼	Shipton-under-Wychwood	Chipping Norton, Withey		•	•	•	•	
15½	6	Charlbury	Oxford, Witney, Chipping Norton	•	•	•	•	•	Private arrangements possible Charlbury
18½	3	Stonesfield	Enstone, Oxford				•	•	
24	5½	Wootton	Oxford, Charlbury, Birmingham, Stratford		•	•	•	•	
28½	4½	Kirtlington	Oxford, Bicester				•	•	
30¾	2¼	Weston-on-the-Green	Oxford, Bicester		•		•	•	Diamond Farm camp site
33¾	3	Islip	Oxford, Bicester			•	•	•	The Lynch, Cherwell Bank
37	3¼	Beckley	—				•		
39	2	Horton-cum-Studley	Oxford			•	•	•	Private arrangements possible, Beckley
46½	7½	Tiddington	Aylesbury, Thame, Oxford			•	•		
50	3½	Tetsworth	Oxford, High Wycombe			•	•	•	
56	6	Pyrton	—				•		
58¾	2¾	Christmas Common	—				•		
61¼	2½	Pishill	—				•		
64½	3¼	Middle Assendon	—				•		
67¼	2¾	Henley-on-Thames	London	•	•	•	•	•	

There are youth hostels at Henley and Charlbury, also Oxford, easily reached by bus from many points, and Stow-on-the-Wold, 5 miles from the start at Bourton-on-the-Water

Two Moors Way

Joe Turner

On 29 May 1976 a Royal Marine helicopter carried a small party across Devon on a unique opening ceremony. Four inscribed blocks of granite were unveiled, at Ivybridge, Drewsteignton, Morchard Bishop, and Lynmouth, proclaiming that the Two Moors Way had formally come into existence. Now this 103 mile footpath route can be followed across Dartmoor and Exmoor, the only two National Parks in the south-west of England, and across the quieter landscapes of mid-Devon between them. But few walkers will realise how many years of work and controversy went into its creation.

This concept of a coast to coast route across the two moorland areas was first planned in 1965 as a bridleway from Plymouth to Lynton. The hard work of planning and surveying was mainly carried out by members of the Ramblers' Association, the YHA and the Dartmoor Preservation Association, and their route was published in 1969. Although the Countryside Commission, the two National Park Committees and most District Councils expressed approval, objections were raised by local landowners and the National Farmers Union. They particularly disliked the idea of a bridleway across mid-Devon, which they wanted to cut out entirely. Faced with this opposition, the Countryside Commission had second thoughts and withdrew its support. No new rights of way would be created for the Two Moors Way, and the whole project seemed doomed.

Then, in some defiance, a new concept was launched by Devon Area of the Ramblers' Association. Our long-distance footpath would use only open moorland, existing rights of way, and minor roads—all ways that we had a perfect right to follow already. When volunteering for this resurveying task, I did not envisage being faced with so many problems. Large areas of northern Dartmoor could not be considered because their use by the military for a firing range meant restricted public access at many times. Also, as the Two Moors Way Committee had always been against the waymarking of the open moor, it was important to find a moorland route we could safely recommend to walkers, when for some this could be the first experience of open, featureless moor.

So the southerly starting point of our route was changed to Ivybridge, thus allowing us to use the disused railway track of Red Lake running northward for 7 miles deep into the open moor, an excellent guide even in bad weather across this remote section. Providing safe crossings over rivers in flood was another problem, and for this reason there are alternative routes in the Exmoor section. In mid-Devon we moved our route further east to find a better network of footpaths, mostly church paths and old drovers' ways, many of which have become minor metalled roads. Surveying this section was not helped by the lack of any clear sign of a footpath on the ground, even when our maps told us that a right of way existed. With the attraction of two National Parks close by, this was an almost forgotten countryside, its paths unused.

Happily at this time, Devon County Council Amenities and Countryside Committee took an interest in our new route. They agreed to adopt, clear and signpost the whole mid-Devon section, the only part they had authority over. The assistance and determination of their Chairman, Councillor Ted Pinney, made up for the lack of support from the National Park authorities. He successfully brought us to that opening ceremony when Charles Ansell, Chairman of Devon County Council, and myself could accompany him in the helicopter on its unique journey.

It has been known for the active walker to complete the route in three days, but as an explorer you will be well advised to allow ten or twelve. You will not be able to resist the temptation to make diversions, especially if you have not visited the National Parks before. In any case, much of the route is hilly so take this into account when planning the distances you intend to walk. Do not expect to find the footpaths easy going. Many of them will introduce you to the rich Devon mud, and the open moor is also liable to be wet, so walking boots are essential.

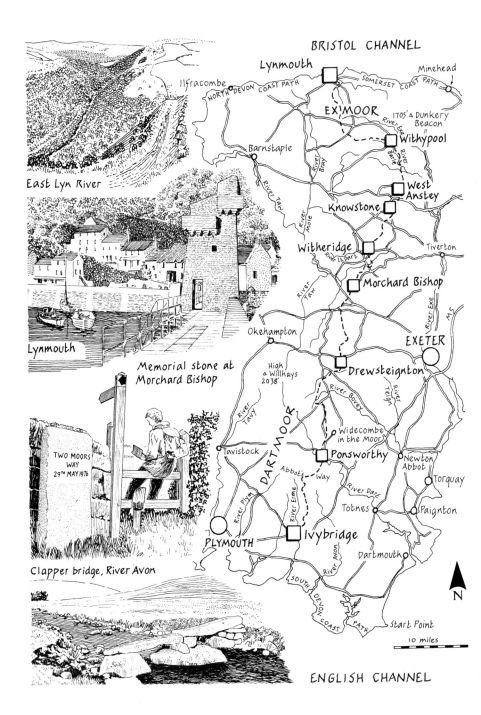

BRISTOL CHANNEL

Lynmouth

Minehead

Ilfracombe

NORTH DEVON COAST PATH

SOMERSET COAST PATH

EXMOOR

1705 ▲ Dunkery
Beacon

River Exe

Withypool

Barnstaple

River Bray

River Barle

West
Anstey

Knowstone

River Mole

River Taw

Witheridge

Tiverton

River Lt Dart

Morchard Bishop

River Taw

River Exe

M5

Okehampton

EXETER

High
▲ Willhays
2038'

Drewsteignton

River Teign

River Bovey

River Taw

DARTMOOR

Widecombe
in the Moor

Tavistock

Ponsworthy

Newton
Abbot

Abbot's Way

River Dart

Torquay

River Plym

River Erme

Totnes

Paignton

PLYMOUTH

Ivybridge

Dartmouth

River Avon

SOUTH DEVON COAST PATH

Start Point

N

10 miles

ENGLISH CHANNEL

East Lyn River

Lynmouth

Memorial stone at
Morchard Bishop

TWO MOORS
WAY
29TH MAY 1976

Clapper bridge, River Avon

The Exmoor Section

The first 28 miles of the Two Moors Way take you over Exmoor, smallest of our National Parks, with varied scenery of grassy plateaux, heather-clad hills, and the steep combes and wooded valleys that fall towards one of the most spectacular coastlines in the south west. Here amongst the oak woods and high bracken you may find the last survivors of the English red deer. The Devonian sedimentary rocks of sandstone, limestone and slate are used locally for building material, adding an extra warmth and contrast to the lovely Exmoor villages.

Lynmouth, the starting point, has been called the Switzerland of England. At the mouth of the Lyn rivers, backed by towering wooded cliffs, is the tiny harbour with its thatched cottages squeezing into the steep-sided valley. You may notice that many of the buildings are new, and the river channel wide and deep. This is to carry the river safely out to sea even in full spate. In a freak summer storm of 1952, the innocent Lyn poured its boulder-laden flood water into little Lynmouth, destroying houses and bridges. Over thirty died that night—disaster in the midst of so much beauty.

The first of the Two Moors Way commemorative stones has been placed opposite the National Park information centre. Enquire here before setting out after a wet spell, to see whether the alternative route might be advisable. Then set off up the lung-testing 700ft climb above Lyn Cleave. On a clear day you will welcome the excuse to linger and admire the awe-inspiring views over the Bristol Channel to Wales and the Brecon Beacons, while far below the East Lyn winds through its wooded valley. After following the zigzag path across Myrtleberry Cleave, a short diversion will reveal the cascades of Watersmeet below, much enhanced if there has been recent rain.

From Hillsford Bridge, the lane beside Farley Water passes through the hamlet of Cheriton and on to the ridge beyond. Lovers of R. D. Blackmoore's *Lorna Doone* could relive some of its romantic pages by diverting to take the walk up beautiful Badgworthy Water with its tributary valleys of Lank Combe and Hoccombe, suggested as the homes of the legendary outlaws. The Two Moors Way can be rejoined at Hoar Oak Tree. But most will keep firmly to the Way, crossing the steep valley of Hoar Oak Water to Stock Common, passing the single-banked, Iron-Age earthwork of Roborough Castle.

Now you are on the open moor, and Hoar Oak Tree marks the ancient Royal Forest boundary, an oak tree having stood here for many centuries. From Norman times until the 1800s, hunting preserves were maintained in the centre of the moor, but today much of the land has been enclosed for grazing. Continuing southward up the Hoar Oak valley, you are in the home of the raven. Its harsh croak will set you searching the sky for the characteristic black outline and deep wedge-shaped tail. In spring they put on quite an acrobatic show, even flying upside down for short distances.

To the west lies the grassy plateau of the Chains, wildest and certainly the wettest area of Exmoor. The Exe and three other rivers rise within a few miles around, and amongst the sedge-covered peat the feeling of solitude is shaken only as you gaze across the source of the Exe to the traffic hurrying along the B3223. Traversing the rough pasture fields to the B3558, you will have reached the highest point on the Exmoor walk, 1525ft up with panoramic views of bare moorland and sky. For overnight accommodation turn east here to Simonsbath, highest village on Exmoor and once the centre of the Royal Forest. The hotel was a hunting lodge during the seventeenth century.

A short way on from the road lies Cornham Ford, a little moorland gem quite unspoilt by visitors, with rolling rounded hills closing it in on all sides. Here you make the first of three crossings of the river Barle. Keep a lookout for the dipper, often seen plunging into the stream, searching the bottom and emerging with a beak full of food—a fascinating sight. Climbing up from the sheltered narrow valleys, the path lies straight ahead across fields where a covey of red grouse or even the spectacular and rare blackcock can be seen hustling with half-closed wings, low over the heather ahead of you.

At Horsen Farm the track descends beside the stream to re-cross the swift-flowing Barle. Above the footbridge in a spur where Barle and White Water meet, lies the prominent mound of Cow Castle, an Iron-Age hill fort. Its defensive banks enclose nearly three acres, beautifully situated and an ideal spot to recline on a hot summer's day and conjecture about the folk who chose such a spot to live, so long ago. From here on, by plantations, pasture land and lanes, the route comes to Withypool. At this small village on the Barle the Forest law was administered until the seventeenth century.

At Withypool you need to decide whether it is safe to follow the valley route, so after heavy rain consult the flood gauge that stands on the upper side of the road bridge. If it reads below 0.5 metres and the water is not rising, keep to the river, otherwise a higher route takes to the slopes of Withypool Hill. If it is the river, the next 3 miles will be most delectable, through the meadows and woods to Tarr Steps. Along the river bank the anglers seem so oblivious to all, they hardly notice that other great fisherman who shares their river, the heron. You may see him standing motionless, knee-deep in water for long periods, seeking the prey which he stabs with a long dagger-shaped bill.

Tarr Steps, the clapper bridge used by Two Moors Way walkers to cross the Barle (*British Tourist Authority*)

Cross the remarkable clapper bridge of Tarr Steps, spanning the river with seventeen stone slabs. Even though these weigh several tons, a great flood in 1952 washed many of the stones down river. It is not easy to put an age to Tarr Steps, but it is most likely to be medieval in origin. Climbing out of the valley to walk beside the cultivated fields of Hawkridge Common, you will get a last glimpse of the Barle beyond South Barton Wood far below. It has been a companion for much of the journey so far—now bid it farewell.

Ahead, Hawkridge village offers welcome accommodation and an interesting twelfth-century church. Then,. as you descend to West Anstey Common, you gain extensive views of the journey ahead, over the gentle rolling fields of mid-Devon to the high tops of Dartmoor in the far distance.

The mid-Devon section

Badlake Moor Cross marks the boundary of Exmoor National Park. Here you will meet the first of the yellow and black arrow markers to be followed through 33 miles of mid-Devon. This countryside differs greatly from the wilderness of the National Park. At times you will have the strange feeling of total isolation in a landscape undiscovered by today's tourist, known only to a local community. It is here that you you are most likely to meet the fox or badger at close quarters. It is a paradise for the ornithologist too, for the many birds that thrive in a land where even today man does not intrude. In its isolated churches and tiny hamlets, you will want to halt awhile without thought of the hour. Time perhaps to stop, talk and gain local knowledge from folk who were born and spent their lives here.

West Anstey, the first settlement you meet, has cottages of colour-washed rubble. The church of St Petrock at its heart has a screen constructed from medieval chamfered joists, while at the back are carved Renaissance bench-ends. Soon you will be entering the Culm Measures of slate, grit and sandstone. The heavy clay and silt underfoot is generally acidic and poorly drained, so dairy and farmstock communities form the landscape around you. Owlaborough Moor offers a short stretch of rough pasture walking where you may be pausing to watch the graceful gliding and soaring of the buzzards that are now a common sight along the Two Moors Way.

Beyond is Knowstone, a village steeped in history. Rest and wander along its narrow street of seventeenth- and eighteenth-century cottages. Or admire the medieval church of St Peter, and look up the tale of its infamous early nineteenth-century rector, John Froude. Locals tell of his ghost still riding the lanes at night.

The remote stretch now to Bradford Bridge is mainly along country roads, so quiet that you could walk it without meeting a single car. The high ground gives extensive views, and the hedgerows are a joy, mainly of beech displaying a wealth of beauty and colour in all seasons. Like many Devon hedges, they are built on a core of stones and packed with turf. A whole world of plants and wild flowers can be found hidden in them, and they have become home to many birds and insects, even providing the passing rambler with a snack of blackberries in autumn. Just before the bridge over the Little Dart, you pass a fine seventeenth-century farmhouse, Bradford Barton, originally a Domesday manor.

Now the valley of the Little Dart will offer shade amongst its trees, time to rest and listen awhile to the gentle sound of water before the path climbs up to Witheridge. This was a Domesday estate, the earliest recorded settlement in mid-Devon, where a weekly market was held in medieval times and a three-day midsummer fair to celebrate the dedication of the parish church, St John the Baptist. The church is of local brown dunstone, and although restored in 1876 it retains an excellent fifteenth-century font and medieval stone pulpit.

The walk to Morchard Bishop undulates over farming uplands, dropping gently to cross numerous small streams which drain towards the river Dalch. The river is crossed near the tiny settlement of Washford Pyne, remote from any busy road. The church of St Paul has a richly carved screen in the old style, another chance to wonder at the work of country craftsmen. Then on by other field paths through farmland that is the true Devon countryside, where you will exchange time of day with few people except local farming folk. In contrast, the silence is harshly broken by the echoing caws from the rookery on Beech Hill. Finally, as you reach welcome refreshment at Morchard

Bishop, you will be greeted by the second of the Two Moors Way stones.

Beyond Morchard Bishop an unavoidable stretch of road walking faces you, including a short tramp along the A377 where fast-moving traffic is a danger. After the main road, two diversions tempt you from the Way: one to Down St Mary with thatched rubble and cob cottages clustered around its village green where you will find food and accommodation; the other is to Copplestone where a Saxon cross at the crossroads tells us how the village came by its name. Standing where it has always stood, the cross is 10ft high of solid granite, elaborately decorated on all four sides. There are only two other such crosses in all Devon.

Clannaborough, back on the Two Moors Way itself, is a small parish with no village. The church is very small, and the rectory has a thatched roof and a fine wood-pillared porch. The geology changes over the next 2 miles, with a narrow zone of permian sandstone extending westwards from Crediton to encroach into the Culm Measures. Now the red soil gives better conditions for arable farming. Our route passes the sixteenth-century Welmstone Barton, rubble and cob with brick chimney stacks and two-storied porch. This was once the manor house and retains traces of its former grandeur.

Webber Lane, an old drovers' track, was cleared in 1978 by an over-enthusiastic council bulldozer, destroying much of its natural beauty and turning it into an uninteresting muddy lane. But nature has a way of forgiving and setting things right, so perhaps time will restore the beauty. At its end comes a fine spot for a picnic. A narrow stream winds its way through the mixed woods of Waterford Plantation and our smallest bird the gold crest, along with the longtailed tit, find the conifers ideal for nesting. Just beyond, the route crosses the Okehampton–Exeter railway and along the embankment, free from spraying and insecticides, many species of butterfly can be seen.

Crossing the rustic bridge over the river Troney, the walk continues by road until, beyond the church of St Andrew at Hittisleigh it takes the line of the church path across the fields and diverts by road bridge to cross the newly constructed A30. You are now entering Dartmoor National Park.

The Dartmoor section

Our final 42 miles cross Dartmoor, the last great wilderness area in southern England. Bleaker and less intimate than the Exmoor scenes of recent memory, it provides over 200 square miles of moorland where we can roam and explore it as a veritable open-air museum of man's existence on earth since 3000 BC. There are over 4,000 visible pre-historic remains, more than any other national park in Europe, besides medieval settlements, long houses, farmsteads and tin mines to remind us of other ages.

A stiff climb leads to the village of Drewsteignton, a perfect composition of thatched cottages and fifteenth-century church. Inside Holy Trinity, look up to the semi-circular wagon roof. Outside you will

Cob and thatch cottages of Drewsteignton, a village passed on the Two Moors Way as it enters Dartmoor National Park (*Leonard and Marjorie Gayton*)

hardly fail to spot the thatched Drewe Arms where Mrs Mudge extends a true Devonshire welcome. Known to all as Aunt Mabel, she has been drawing ale from the barrel for almost sixty years. Leave the village to pass the third of the Two Moors Way stones. As you approach the romantically named Hunters' Path, the steep tree-clad Teign gorge unfolds before you, with the fast-flowing river far below. Across the valley you could be fortunate to see fallow deer in the woods, Dartmoor's only native stock. Even higher above the gorge is Cranbrook Castle, an Iron-Age fort with stone-faced inner ramparts commanding a superb view. Two other fine hill forts, .Prestonbury and Wooston, lie on each side of the gorge a little further east.

Anyone wanting to walk by the river can drop down the path to the seventeenth-century Fingle Bridge, one of Devon's beauty spots, then along the Fisherman's Path on the north of the Teign. Our route follows the Hunters' Path high along the gorge with delightful views all around and over the patchwork fields to the journey ahead. To the north stands Castle Drogo, its imposing solid granite walls both arrogant and romantic. Owned now by the National Trust, it was created by Sir Edwin Lutyens for the Drewe family, founders of the Home and Colonial Stores. Surely the last castle to be built in England!

Coming to the river valley, the geology changes for the last time to Dartmoor granite. The next few miles are pleasant walking by the Teign, in summer a chance to watch the common Blue Damsel Fly whose short adult life adds a flash of colour to the river scene. Swimming is possible during summer months in the open-air pool at Rushford Mill but be warned—moorland water is much colder than sea water!

Chagford, reached along the river, was until 1749 one of the stannary towns to which the tinners brought their metal for weighing and stamping. The busy little place still has much of interest and many of the houses are of early date. The Three Crowns Hotel is a mullioned and gabled building of thirteenth-century origins, and it is reputed that the young poet Sidney Godolphin was killed by Cromwell's men in the porchway. In the centre of the town stands an octagonal Victorian market house, while if you happen to want the local Lloyds Bank, look for a pretty thatched cottage in the square. Chagford welcomes its visitors with flowers, and in 1968 the little town won the Britain in Bloom competition.

A lane leads on along the Teign valley to Teigncombe. Here hostellers will turn off northwards to the little hostel at Gidleigh, while the Two Moors Way joins a much older path, the Mariners' Way, originally tramped out by seamen passing from Bideford to Dartmouth. Only the Dartmoor section of this way is now traceable, where it skirts the eastern flank of the high moor to link up farms and hamlets that provided food and somewhere to spend the night. At Yardworthy just such a farm can be seen, a medieval farmhouse with porch of massive granite blocks.

Crossing Chagford Common you will meet the first stretch of open moorland where there are no waymarks or tracks to follow and a compass is essential. Amongst the tussocks and moorland heather, the skylark and meadow pipit build their nests, soaring skywards as you approach and filling the air with music. In the hollow of the common is a good example of a double stone row 450ft in length, a processional way leading to a cairn at the southern end. Tramping the ridge around dusk in autumn or winter, you will be able to witness a truly spectacular

A prehistoric stone row on Chagford Common, Dartmoor (*J. R. Turner*)

sight as the starlings fly along their familiar flight paths to roost in Soussons Plantation. They fly in from all directions in groups of up to a thousand, timing their arrival so that each group settles with the minimum of fuss. Who decides which group shall arrive first and from which direction? Numbers may reach a million in some winters.

Bennetts Cross marks our approach to the Princetown road, a weathered 6ft granite cross with the letter WB carved on the face. They stand for Warren Boundary, thus defining the old boundary between Headland Warren and North Bovey. Viewing the valley scene to the south, it is difficult to visualise it a hundred years ago when over a hundred men worked at Birch Tor and Vitaford tin mines. The area was worked up to and between the two world wars. On either side of the valley deep trenches scar the skyline, while the remains of buildings, wheel pits and dressing floors are still visible. Water power for washing and dressing came here by a winding $7\frac{1}{2}$ mile leat from the East Dart river. On the road south-west is the remote Warren House Inn.

Now crossing the saddle between Hookney Tor and Hamel Down we pass the well-preserved remains of Grimspound, the rough circular drystone wall enclosing over twenty stone huts of a Bronze-Age village. The roofs were of wood and turf, long decayed away, but the granite walls stand for century after century here on the open moor. Climbing the whale-back ridge of Hamel Down brings the Way to its highest point at 1700ft. For over a mile along the ridge our path stays level with magnificent views all around. Princetown is easily located by the high television mast on North Hessary Tor. This bleak moorland town has an even more sinister appearance at night when the austere buildings of the prison are illuminated like some faraway seaside resort. This heather-clad ridge gives ideal cover for the red grouse through spring and summer, and the hunting cry of the curlew adds its evocative touch. Along this same path 3,000 years ago came the people from the settlements below to bury their dead in round barrows covered with heather and grass, beneath which the ashes were placed under stone slabs. When the more northerly of the Two Barrows was excavated a century ago, the blade of a grooved Bronze-Age dagger was discovered, along with an amber pommel studded with gold pins. Alas, they went to Plymouth Museum and were destroyed in an air raid.

St. Pancras, Widecombe-in-the-Moor

Bennett's Cross, Headland Warren

Now you will be looking down towards Widecombe-in-the-Moor, a famous view with grey granite houses deeply set in their green valley. The church of St Pancras with its high granite tower and crocketed pinnacles is often referred to as the cathedral of the moor. Just within the church is an inscribed verse, telling of the day in October 1639 when the tower was struck by lightning during a service. Masonry fell into the nave, killing four parishioners and injuring over sixty, mainly from burns. Interesting houses include Church House, once an almshouse and a good example of local moorstone. Also Glebe House, now a gift shop but formerly an 86 acre farm from which past vicars gained their living. But pride of place on the green goes to the modern stone-carved monument to Uncle Tom Cobley, immortalised in the song. He is said to have borrowed an old grey mare to travel from his home in nearby Spreyton to Widecombe Fair, and to this very day a fair is held on the second Tuesday of September, bringing thousands to this little village.

The way on to New Bridge skirts the high moor, passing Jordan, a typical ancient Dartmoor settlement, and Pondsworthy with its lovely granite and thatch cottages and a stream running gently across a shallow ford. New Bridge spans the river Dart with three grey arches and pointed buttresses, probably the oldest road bridge on the moor, being 'new' when replaced in the fifteenth century. Ahead, our way follows the valley of Cleave Wood, where the Dart forms deep pools and miniature waterfalls. Tempting here to linger and enjoy the sounds of water, the sunlight filtering through the trees, and maybe to watch the local canoeists at their sport. Leaving the Dart, the path climbs to Holne, a delightful village with commanding views of the river valley, a fourteenth-century church and welcoming Church House Inn.

Having come by green lanes to the wooden footbridge over the Mardle at Chalk Ford, the way ahead covers some nine miles of open moorland, climbing to 1500ft at its highest point. At this height a mist can descend very quickly, so unless the weather is reliably fine do not proceed without suitable clothing and provisions. It is possible to take any number of routes southwards, but you will get the best views by following the ridge top via Huntingdon Warren, Peter's Cross, Three Barrows and Butterdon Hill. The official line of the path climbs along a grassy strip surrounded by high bracken in summer, with scattered hawthorn and mountain ash, finally coming into tufted grass and heather before it reaches Hickaton Hill. Over the summit on the side of a hill is a group of grassy mounds that may set you thinking. They are the remains of Huntingdon Warren, once a thriving 600 acre rabbit farm. The rectangular mounds were built for the rabbits to live in. Here they were encouraged to breed during the summer and were trapped in winter as a convenient supply of fresh meat. The now-dry leat with its little bridges to allow the rabbits to cross, can be traced to the river Avon.

In 1909, the botanist Keeble Martin, later to become the Rev Keeble Martin, left his traces on the moorland hereabouts. Between a ramp that served a nineteenth-century wheel pit and the Western Wella Brook, he built a tiny grotto known locally as Keeble Martin's Church.

The Dart in its wooded valley below New Bridge (*Leonard and Marjorie Gayton*)

A little stone enclosure has a raised section at the north end where a granite pillar is inscribed with a cross. As a youth he spent many days camping on the moor and must have found deep inspiration in studying and drawing the array of grasses, ferns, blanket bog, heathers and wild flowers—the sun dew, bog asphodel, bog bean, marsh violet and others that grow in abundance here.

Crossing the Avon by a granite clapper, the next mile of the walk follows the Abbot's Way, a moorland track said to have linked the abbeys of Buckfast in the east with Buckland in the west. Coming to Crossways, we reach the disused rail track that will complete our journey. Here the wild aspect of the moor unfolds. To the north lies Red Lake, the china-clay workings that the old tramway served. Among these remote workings the Canada goose with its striking black head and white chin patch has been known to raise its family, and in the dry summer months the cattle and ponies will gather at Red Lake Pool. The Dartmoor pony is neat and compact, with a handsome head much smaller than its Exmoor neighbour. They are left to graze over their vast territory all year round, but once a year the young ponies are rounded up and driven off the moor to be sold at various markets. The cattle on the high moor are mostly the hardy Scottish breeds, Galloways and Highlands. The horns of the Highland cattle give them a ferocious appearance, but they are both gentle and docile.

Now the old track provides a sure guide even in poor visibility. Westward along the Erme valley are many prehistoric monuments including an exceptional stone row over 2 miles long, starting from a ring cairn to cross the Erme and ending at a cairn on Green Hill. Further south along the valley, Piles Copse is one of three surviving indigenous oak woods within the National Park. The dwarf trees, their growth restricted by climate, are covered with lichen and ferns. Rounding the western flank of Weatherdon Hill, the view south is rewarding. On a clear day you will be looking over the farmlands of the South Hams and along the English Channel to Plymouth and Cornwall. Dropping down from the open moor, the lane will bring you, just after a railway bridge, to the last of the Two Moors Way stones. Ahead is Ivybridge beside the Erme, journey's end.

Two Moors Way

Progressive Mileage	Miles Between	Places on route	Bus service to	Rail Service	Cafes	Accommodation	Inns providing snacks etc	Shops	Camping
-	-	Lynmouth	Barnstaple, Ilfracombe		●	●	●	●	
12	12	Simonsbath	—			●	●		
20	8	Withypool	—		●	●	●	●	
26	6	Hawkridge	—		●	●			
28	2	West Anstey	—			●			There are no official camp sites, but farmers will usually allow a small tent if you ask permission first.
32	4	Knowstone	—			●		●	
39	7	Witheridge	South Molton, Exeter		●	●	●	●	
46	7	Morchard Bishop	Exeter, Bideford	●		●	●	●	
49	3	Down St Mary	—			●	●	●	
61	12	Drewsteignton	Okehampton, Newton Abbot, Exeter			●	●	●	
65	4	Chagford	Okehampton, Exeter		●	●	●	●	
73	8	Bennetts Cross Warren House Inn	Plymouth, Mortonhampstead				●		
80	7	Widecombe-in-the-Moor	Bovey Tracey		●	●	●	●	
83	3	Pondsworthy	—			●			
88	5	Holne	—		●	●	●	●	
103	15	Ivybridge	Plymouth, Exeter		●	●	●	●	

There are youth hostels at Lynton, Withypool, Gidleigh and Bellever

Early closing: Wednesday afternoon at Hawkridge and Chagford. Thursday afternoon at Lynton, Withypool, Hawkridge and Morchard Bishop

National Express buses from London serve Lynton (for Lynmouth) and Ivybridge

The Cumbria Way

John Trevelyan

The concept of the Way began with the work put in by members of the Ramblers' Association North Cumbria Group, based on Carlisle, in making the paths of the Caldew valley usable again after years of neglect. One of the features of the path network in the valley is the ability to walk close to the river virtually all the way from the centre of Carlisle to Caldbeck, on the edge of the Lake District National Park. Having decided to give this walk some publicity, we then had the idea of extending it into and through the heart of the Lake District to Morecambe Bay on the further side. At the time these thoughts were taking shape, local government reorganisation was about to merge the old counties of Cumberland and Westmorland, together with parts of Lancashire and the West Riding of Yorkshire, to form Cumbria. The route we finally decided on traversed all three major constituent parts of the new county, so naturally we borrowed its name. The Cumbria Way it had to be.

The southern approach to Lakeland from Ulverston was devised by the Association's Furness Group, and the central section through Great Langdale and Borrowdale was planned as a valley walk, to keep off the roads as far as possible and provide an easy and enjoyable way to see some of the best of the heart of Lakeland. A second aim in planning the line of the Way was to provide walking routes away from roads to link the major centres of Ulverston, Coniston, Keswick, Caldbeck and Carlisle. By a short walk from Skelwith Bridge over the side of Loughrigg Fell, Ambleside could be added to the list of centres thus linked.

In all, the 75 miles of the Way cover a good variety of Cumbrian scenery, from the placid shores of Coniston Water, via the soaring crags of the Langdale Pikes and the wild openness of the northern fells,

N

5 miles

Carlisle
River Eden
M6

Dalston

Sebergham

Caldbeck
Hesket Newmarket

Over Water
High Pike
Dash Falls
Skiddaw Forest
Mosedale
Bassenthwaite Lake
Skiddaw
Blencathra

Dash Falls

Keswick
Derwent Water
Catbells
Thirlmere
Jaws of Borrowdale
Rosthwaite
Helvellyn
Honister Pass
Dunmail Raise
Scafell Pike
Stake Pass
Langdale Pikes
Grasmere
Scafell
Bowfell
Great Langdale
River Esk
Wrynose Pass
Elterwater
Ambleside

Yewdale

Yewdale
Tarn Hows
Coniston Old Man
Coniston
Coniston Water
Torver
Grisedale
Windermere
River Duddon
Beacon Tarn

Coniston Water

Ulverston

to the gently pastoral Caldew valley. In busy Great Langdale, the Way keeps clear of the valley roads and follows the water's edge for much of the valley. Again, in Borrowdale the excellent network of footpaths is used to avoid roads that often take streams of motorised visitors. North of Keswick, the only town of any size along the Way, the route contours high above the Glenderaterra valley to enter its most wild and open section. Here, because the Way generally is designed to provide an easy walk, an alternative route avoids the climb over the 2000ft line and instead skirts around the high ground and provides an opportunity to visit Dash Falls and Bassenthwaite village.

The Cumbria Way is not intended simply as a tramp through the Lake District, but rather as an introduction to the scenery of the region, and to the many and fascinating paths to be found on its fringes. Even some Lakes enthusiasts who are familiar with the mountain tops but not with the valley paths, will find that a walk along all or part of the Way reveals new aspects. A reasonably fit and able walker should be able to manage 15 miles in a day, so, taking only five days along the Way itself, you could complete a full week's holiday by spending a couple of extra nights at favourite centres. By a little fell walking, you would be viewing the valleys from above, as well as the fells from below.

The Way divides easily into five days of around 15 miles each, with stops at Coniston, Dungeon Ghyll, Keswick and Caldbeck. For someone aiming to walk only 10 miles a day, I would divide the route into sections ending at Sunny Bank (bus to Torver or Coniston), Elterwater, Stonethwaite or Rosthwaite, Keswick, Bassenthwaite and Caldbeck or Sebergham. If you have a willing car driver to meet you and take you on to Caldbeck, then the end of the road up Mosedale by the Carrock Mine could be substituted for Bassenthwaite on the list. The section from Caldbeck to Carlisle is easiest of all and, with the excellent rail services out of Carlisle, it is perfectly feasible to leave Caldbeck promptly after breakfast, walk on to Carlisle and be home the same evening, even if home is several hundred miles away.

A few points to remember before you start out along the Cumbria Way. Firstly, you can find accommodation at numerous points along the route, but bear in mind though that between Coniston and Keswick it is much in demand on summer weekends. To reach the start, Ulverston is on the rail line from Lancaster to Barrow-in-Furness, with approximately an hourly service. There are connections at Lancaster or Preston for services south and north, and an eastward link to Leeds via Carnforth. About every three hours, a train runs beyond Barrow along the coast to Carlisle, a scenic if slow journey. Carlisle with no less than six rail services and a location on the main London to Glasgow rail route, enjoys excellent communications. Along the Way, bus services are provided by Ribble Motor Services out of Ulverston, Ambleside and Caldbeck, Mountain Goat from Windermere and Ambleside, and Cumberland Motor Services out of Keswick. Few buses run on Sundays but services generally are more frequent in summer. It could also be worth remembering the Derwentwater ferry too, from Brandlehow to Keswick. As for equipment, the Lakeland paths are often stony underfoot and for comfort as well as safety, boots should be worn on this walk. The only other essential items to take are those needed to keep out wind and rain, for, as all lovers of the Lakeland scene will know very well, both may be encountered at any time of year.

Ulverston to Coniston

Ulverston, at the southern end of the Cumbria Way, is a small market town close to the shores of Morecambe Bay. It is just as well perhaps, that it has all the facilities needed to prepare the walker for his trip, for the first section of the Way is bereft of shops or pubs until Coniston is reached. Near the town centre is the Gill, a large square used as a car park, and in the western corner a path leads off beside a beck. The path is the beginning of the Cumbria Way, and the water is Gillbanks Beck from which Ulverston's mills used to derive their power. Beyond the wooded section along the gill, the Way climbs into farmland and the town is soon left behind. After a mile, a steep slope is climbed past Bortree Stile, and there are excellent views of Morecambe Bay with the Forest of Bowland and Ingleborough visible in the distance. The Way then returns to the valley, with views of Kirkby Moor ahead. Through kissing gates, a field path takes the walker to the Victorian Osmotherley parish church, from which there are the first good views northward to the Scafell range and the Coniston fells.

Beyond the church, the Way drops to the small village of Broughton Beck, then follows a beck leading eventually to the edge of Lowick Common. Instead of crossing the common though, the Way climbs north-west to the hamlet of Gawthwaite on the southern edge of the National Park. The track leading north from Gawthwaite gives excellent views of the Coniston Fells and Coniston Water below them, before descending to pass High Stennerley Farm. From here to Beacon Tarn, the Way follows a variety of tracks and paths, some clear, some indistinct, over increasingly rough country. Beacon Tarn, reached by a stiff climb from Cocken Skell, is a real gem, not least because it is accessible only on foot and lies away from central Lakeland. It is certainly a most pleasant place to rest awhile, and not being too far from Ulverston makes the ideal spot for a late lunch.

The view from the Cumbria Way to Tarn Hows Cottage, with Coniston Old Man cloud-capped in the background (*Geoffrey Berry*)

The Tarn, and the land crossed by the Way ahead as far as the first camp site on Coniston Water, form part of the Torver commons, now owned by the National Park Planning Board and open to the public so that you may roam at will. Just before the Ulverston–Coniston road is reached at Sunny Bank, Torver Beck must be crossed by stepping stones—there is a rope to help you. Across the road the path climbs briefly before descending to Coniston Water and following the shoreline north. Coniston Water is the largest lake on the Cumbria Way, and there are fine views along the lake and across to the eastern shore, close to which lies the former home of the painter Ruskin at Brantwood, now a museum. There is also a small Ruskin museum in Coniston village. Beyond the sixteenth-century Coniston Hall, the Way heads inland across the fields to the village. Situated between the fells and the lake, Coniston has a real feeling of being in the heart of Lakeland, although it still has a strong industrial base in slate quarrying.

Coniston to Skelwith Bridge

The next section of the Way is in sharp contrast to the broken terrain of the country we have crossed south of Coniston. Here are the high and rugged Coniston Fells, but below them the wooded slopes above Yewdale and Little Langdale. To the north are views of the Langdale Pikes and Grisedale Hause. On leaving Coniston, the Way climbs the slopes of High Guards with a fine view back down to the lake, before returning to Yewdale Beck at Low Yewdale. From the bridge a path climbs through the National Trust's Tarn Hows Wood, in part following a forest road, to reach Tarn Hows Cottage. Here you are high above the Coniston–Ambleside road, looking down on Yew Tree farm, one of the few Lakeland farms to retain its spinning gallery. From the cottage, the road is followed to the Tarns, better known as Tarn Hows, and one of the most photographed and visited places in the Lake District.

The western shore of the Tarns is followed through woodland to the main road, to take a minor road along the edge of Tongue Intake plantation down to High Park overlooking Little Langdale. Here a change of direction leads to an easterly path through another National

The Langdale Pikes from Tarn Hows

Trust wood, where the Trust has kindly provided an excellent alternative to enable visitors to see Colwith Force, a magnificent waterfall, without having to retrace their steps. Continuing to Skelwith Bridge, the Way follows a well-used path with some fine views north across the meeting of the two Langdales to Elterwater.

Skelwith Bridge to Stake Pass

At the bridge the Way follows a path on the north bank of the river, passing through the slate workshops and display area to reach Skelwith Force, another attractive fall although not as high as Colwith. Beyond the Force the path passes through meadows and woodlands on the edge of Elterwater, probably more accurately described as a large tarn than as a lake, and there is now an alternative riverside path for the last $\frac{1}{4}$ mile to the village. Here the route crosses the bridge and follows the quarry road for a short way before climbing down opposite a large cavern to cross the river once more. In fact, in its journey up the valley, the Way crosses all the available bridges as far as Side House Farm. On the opposite side of the water at this point is the former Elterwater gunpowder works, now a holiday centre.

A short journey past the Langdales Hotel and through Thrang farm leads back to the river again with a fine single-span arch bridge, and the walker takes a riverside path for a mile or more, eventually turning away to climb above the intake wall, with fine views of the Langdale Pikes on the northern side of the dale. After descending to Side House Farm, the beck is crossed for the final time and the Way goes round behind the two Dungeon Ghyll hotels, passing beneath the crags so beloved of rock climbers, and out into the open expanse of Mickleden with its fine collection of moraines. Up above, in amongst the crags,

Great Langdale from above Harry Place. The Way follows the river Brathay in the dale bottom past New Dungeon Ghyll Hotel, seen at the foot of the Langdale Pikes
(*Geoffrey Berry*)

have been found traces of a Neolithic axe factory whose wares are known to have been sent all over Britain. It seems a reasonable conclusion that the tracks at the head of Great Langdale, leading up and over Rossett Gill and Stake Pass, were used by those early folk transporting their axes, since specimens have been discovered on the seaward side of the western dales. Possibly then, some of the paths the Way follows here have been in use for the past 5,000 years.

At the head of Mickleden the route climbs the northern side of the dale to reach Stake Pass at a height of over 1500ft. Stake Pass can be regarded as halfway point along the Way, although to be strictly accurate this occurs 6 miles further north between Rosthwaite and Grange. The pass not only links the two major valleys, but also forms an important watershed. Until now all the river flow has been eventually southwards to the shores of Morecambe Bay, either via Coniston Water or Windermere, but from now on it all flows north or west into Solway Firth via the Derwent, Ellen or Caldew.

Stake Pass to Keswick

The Way descends from the pass by the side of Stake Beck, which forms some fine cascades and inviting pools. Down in the valley the beck is crossed but the path keeps to the eastern side of Langstrath all the way down. The valley is fine and wild with towering crags on either side, and all the better for not having a road through it. However it does not lead as directly to Borrowdale as may at first be supposed, but joins, almost at right angles, a side valley coming down from Greenup Gill, and this leads straight to the main valley of Borrowdale. Looking back from Stonethwaite, it is hard to believe that a side valley carves several miles into the central core of the fells, so sharply is it cut off. At the junction with Greenup Gill, the Way joins another long-distance route, the Coast to Coast Walk, on its east–west journey across Lakeland, and together the two Ways share the journey to Rosthwaite, the centre of upper Borrowdale with pubs, a shop and a certain amount of accommodation. Its location on ground raised just above the valley

Along the rocky Langstrath Beck, the Cumbria Way takes the right bank (*Geoffrey Berry*)

floor was a deliberate choice of the early settlers, who saw in the flat valley bottom an area of potential flooding. The flatness of this bottom, the site of a former lake as in Langdale, is in sharp contrast to the cliffs of Castle Crag a short distance to the north, where the Jaws of Borrowdale almost seal off the valley from its northward continuation.

After climbing the slopes of Castle Crag to squeeze through the Jaws, the Way keeps above Grange village by taking a track through Hollows Farm. The farm marks the boundary between two distinctive landscape types—the rough, rugged crags of the Borrowdale volcanic series, a feature of the countryside along the Way from Coniston onwards, and the much smoother slopes and ridges of the Skiddaw slates, most noticeable in the views ahead of Catbells and of the Skiddaw range in the distance beyond Derwentwater. Our route soon descends to the

Into Borrowdale, with Glaramara beyond, the Cumbria Way passes through the valley hamlet of Rosthwaite (*Geoffrey Berry*)

lake shore and passes through Brandelhow woods, one of the first-ever acquisitions of the National Trust, on its route to Portinscale and Keswick, between which can be found a fine modern suspension footbridge. Keswick owes much of its current prosperity to tourism and provides just about everything the walker on the Way might need. But in earlier times it was a centre for the mining activities of the district, and the Moot Hall Information Centre and the Museum in Station Road can both tell more of this story.

Keswick to Caldbeck

The country north of Keswick may not conform to your idea of typical Lakeland scenery. There are no lakes and few crags or trees, indeed in many ways it is more reminiscent of the Cheviots or of parts of Scotland, but it is nevertheless grand open country, mostly over the 1000ft line with a real sense of solitude, and a good contrast to the adjoining areas both to the north and south. Leaving the town, the Way skirts the slopes of Latrigg, the summit of which may easily be reached by a slight detour. From here a most splendid and wide-ranging view can be enjoyed with the narrow ridges of the fells to the west of Borrowdale seen to particular advantage. The Way then skirts Lonscale Fell, part of the Skiddaw massif, to enter the steep valley of the Glenderaterra situated on a faultline which can be seen running south over Dunmail Raise to Grasmere and beyond.

The northern fells are divided into three groups, separated by the valleys of the Caldew river and the Dash and Glenderaterra becks. At the centre of all this loneliness lies Skiddaw House, an old shepherd's house now used as an outdoor centre by a Carlisle school, with one room available as an open shelter for all who pass by. Beyond the house there are two alternatives. The direct route to Caldbeck lies over the fells ahead, but if this sounds too demanding or if the weather makes such a traverse unattractive, there is an easier option. This lies straight ahead along a clear track which soon drops into a cultivated valley. The beck also drops—over the aptly named Whitewater Dash or Dash Falls. Down in the valley the track leads to Peterhouse Farm and beyond to Bassenthwaite village, which might serve as a place to stay the night,

or to catch a bus to return to Keswick. The Way itself only goes a short
distance beyond Peterhouse before heading north past Little Tarn,
Orthwaite and Overwater to follow tracks both rough and metalled in
its skirting of the fells. Such metalled roads as are followed are normally
quiet, and this alternative generally provides easy all-weather walking.

Back at Skiddaw House, the direct route heads north–east for the
valley of the Caldew and follows a steadily improving track for 3 miles
down river to the beginnings of a metalled road. Here a sharp turn is
made to go north–west up the valley of the Grainsgill Beck, through
the mine workings and up to a hut on the skyline on the slopes of Great
Lingy Hill, heather-clad as the name suggests. From the hut a clear
track leads northwards, but it is left after a mile to visit the summit of
High Pike, most northerly of the Lakeland peaks at over 2000ft.
Because of its location, it enjoys splendid views in a wide arc from the
south–western tip of Scotland across to the Cheviots and down the
Pennines towards the Yorkshire Dales. Nearer at hand lies the North
Cumbria plain, Caldbeck and the Caldew valley, down which our
walk follows the river to Carlisle. The route off High Pike due north to
Nether Row and Caldbeck passes old mine workings which one
hundred years ago supported a population twice the size of present-day
Caldbeck. The village is an attractive one with shops, a pub and
accommodation. In the churchyard can be found the tomb of John Peel
of 'coat so grey', and in the Howk, a limestone gorge to the west of the
village, are the remains of an old mill, well worth a visit on an evening
stroll.

Caldbeck to Carlisle

The final section of the route passes through gentle pastoral countryside
and provides an easy finale to the walk. All the way, there are fine
views back to High Pike and the adjoining fells, and across to the
North Pennines. A woodland walk from Caldbeck leads above and
then alongside the river to Sebergham Bridge. Across the bridge, a path
leads up to the church and then north past the hall to return to the river
at Bell Bridge. For the next 3 miles the western bank of the river is
followed, until Rose Bridge is reached. From the Way near the

bridge, there is an excellent general view of Rose Castle, seat of the Bishops of Carlisle for many centuries. For a closer inspection, a public footpath leads off from the bridge right round the outside of the Castle grounds. The Way proper heads north to the Georgian Hawksdale Hall before reaching Buckabank. Here Dalston Parish Council has recently opened up a new riverside walk on the eastern bank to the high single-span bridge just below the mill track. The way through the mill follows the leat on to White Bridge, now closed to traffic and giving access to the centre of Dalston village.

On leaving the village, the Way skirts two schools and a factory before following the railway line along the wide valley to Cummersdale. Here we part company with the railway but not with the river, and the skyline of Carlisle is seen clearly for the first time. Water from the Caldew powered many of Carlisle's textile mills, some of which are still to be seen from the Way as it makes tracks for the city centre. When it finally leaves the river there is less than half a mile of road-walking before the stations and shops are reached.

Walks along the Way

The Cumbria Way can provide a whole range of short, easy walks along the Lakeland dales. Some suggestions would be Sunny Bank to Coniston, Skelwith Bridge to Dungeon Ghyll, Rosthwaite to Grange, or Grange to Keswick, all around 5 miles, with a return to your starting point by bus in each case. Or if you prefer to spend a few days at centres along the route to do more path and fell exploring, there are several good booklets to guide you, produced by or for the Ramblers' Association. Walks south of Stake Pass are featured in the booklet *Park your car and take a walk II*, by the Association's Furness Group, and also in *Walking in Central Lakeland* by Brian and Jay Greenwood. A companion volume *Walking in Northern Lakeland* by Peter Lewis and Brian Porter gives similar coverage to the Way and nearby paths around Borrowdale and Keswick.

The Cumbria Way

Progressive Mileage	Miles Between	Places on route	Bus service to	Rail Service	Cafes	Accommodation	Inns providing snacks etc	Shops	Camping
-	-	Ulverston	Kendal, Windermere	●	●	●	●	●	
5½	5½	Gawthwaite	Ulverston, Millom						
12	6½	Sunny Bank	Ulverston, Coniston			●			
16½	4½	Coniston	Ulverston, Skelwith, Ambleside		●	●	●	●	●
23	6½	Skelwith Bridge	Coniston, Ambleside, Langdale		●	●	●		
25	2	Elterwater	Ambleside, Dungeon Ghyll		●	●	●		●
29	4	Dungeon Ghyll	Ambleside		●	●			●
37	8	Rosthwaite	Keswick, Grange		●	●	●		●
39½	2½	Grange	Keswick, Rosthwaite			●			●
43½	4	Portinscale	Keswick		●	●	●	●	
45	1½	Keswick	Ambleside, Carlisle, Borrowdale, Penrith		●	●	●	●	●
56	11	Bassenthwaite (alt. route)	Carlisle, Keswick		●	●	●		●
61	5	Caldbeck	Carlisle, Dalston		●	●	●	●	
71	10	Dalston	Carlisle, Caldbeck	●	●	●	●	●	
76	5	Carlisle	Keswick, Caldbeck, Dalston, Bassenthwaite, Penrith	●	●	●	●	●	

There are youth hostels at Coniston Far End, Elterwater, Longthwaite, and Keswick, with hostels convenient for the end points in Carlisle and at Arnside, a 25 minute train ride from Ulverston.

Note: Bassenthwaite to Caldbeck by the alternative route, is 10 miles

The North Bucks, Grafton and Knightley Ways

Jean Jefcoate

Beyond the Chiltern escarpment lies the lower land of the Vale of Aylesbury and north Buckinghamshire, little known and unexplored country when compared with the popular hills to the south. In consequence, until a few years ago the network of paths in the Vale showed all the symptoms of long neglect. We appealed for people to come and help to make these rights of way useable again, and as a result a few stalwarts were enlisted and each given a number of parishes to work on. Naturally they met together from time to time, to discuss achievements and problems. All were aware that they were enjoying some very pleasant countryside during their 'work' and wondered how to encourage others to venture forth into the area. Why not a long-distance path, to lure ramblers down from the Chiltern heights and out into the unknown Vale?

The idea caught on immediately, and with maps spread out a route was plotted to incorporate many of the high spots between starting and finishing points that could be reached by public transport. The distance between the two points was 30 miles—perhaps a weekend's walk. Each member of the little footpaths team was responsible for writing up a description of a section of the route, although several surveyed it together. This way, they could be sure that the proper line of path was being followed, and problems were easier to deal with. Negotiating a barbed wire fence is a lesser hazard if someone is there to help, and there is safety in numbers if faced by a landowner who has seldom seen anyone on his land before! Many letters were sent to the county council asking for signposts to be erected, obstructions to be removed, and arrangements made for our work team to reinstate missing footbridges over Buckinghamshire streams and ditches.

We soon decided that, like its bigger and 'official' relations, the North Bucks Way should be waymarked. A large yellow arrow was selected as the waymark, but it took two years to gain permission from the many landowners involved to mark the public paths over their land. In all 30 miles, only one landowner refused permission, even though the whole route is on public rights of way.

Contrary to first impressions, the Vale of Aylesbury is not completely flat, for there are little hills which afford fine views and which, over a day's walking, can add up to a fair amount of climbing. Much of the land is agricultural but there is ample woodland and hedgerows, many free-running and sparkling brooks fed by numerous springs, the villages with their pretty gardens, thatched cottages and a heritage of fine churches. The air is clean with a tang of its own. In summer it has the mellowness of ripening crops, and in winter the freshness that seems to suggest snow-capped mountains. However long you spend on the Way, a day or several, it will be a tonic.

All tastes are catered for, from the avid walker and those seeking peace and beauty to the specialists—botanist, ornithologist, geologist or historian. A few day's escape, and even the worry of route-finding in this intricate countryside has been much relieved by the waymarking. Transport, alas, is not as plentiful as it was in the early 1900s when several railway lines crossed the north of Buckinghamshire, but with a little planning around timetables this presents no problem.

The North Buckinghamshire Way

The route starts on Chequers Knap high on the Chiltern escarpment above Great Kimble. It is possible to reach the path leading to the Knap by bus from Aylesbury or High Wycombe, or you could walk along the Upper Icknield Way, now followed by the official Ridgeway Path; the two routes intersect by the Knap. Nearby is Chequers Court, the country residence of the Prime Minister, not open to the public. On a clear day the view from the escarpment is extensive, and the first high spot on the route, Waddesdon, can be seen to the north with the manor now partly visible because trees have been felled. Wittenham

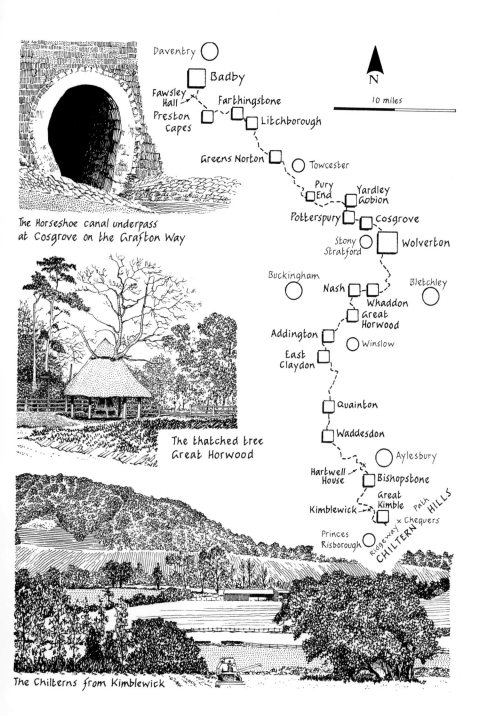

Daventry

Badby

Fawsley
Hall

Farthingstone

Preston
Capes

Litchborough

Greens Norton

Towcester

Pury
End

Yardley
Gobion

Potterspury

Cosgrove

Stony
Stratford

Wolverton

Buckingham

Nash

Bletchley

Whaddon

Great
Horwood

Addington

Winslow

East
Claydon

Quainton

Waddesdon

Aylesbury

Hartwell
House

Bishopstone

Great
Kimble

Path
HILLS

Kimblewick

x Chequers

Princes
Risborough

CHILTERN

Ridgeway Path

N

10 miles

The Horseshoe canal underpass
at Cosgrove on the Grafton Way

The thatched tree
Great Horwood

The Chilterns from Kimblewick

Waddesdon Manor and deer park, seen from the North Bucks Way (*C. Martland*)

Clumps in Oxfordshire are to the west, whilst two other Rothschild residences, Mentmore and Halton, might be spotted to the east.

Leaving the escarpment, Great Kimble church is just below, standing on a little knoll with its medieval tower. It was here that an eminent son of Bucks, John Hampden, made his protest against Ship Money in defiance of Charles I. Nearby at the Old Grange farmhouse is a field with the grass-covered remains of an earlier and much larger village of Kimble. Crossing the Lower Icknield Way, the summer route of prehistoric travellers along the escarpment, our Way comes to a tiny community with the name of Dodd's Charity. It is probably named after the gift of almshouses at nearby Ellesborough made by Dame Dodd in a will dated 2 March 1746. Although it may be unlucky to look back whilst traversing these fields, there is a temptation here to view the long line of the Chilterns to the south.

Soon the first hamlet is reached, Bishopstone, and here are half-timbered and thatched cottages. One has straw pheasants on its roof, the thatcher's trademark! After crossing the A418 the village of Hart-well appears round a corner, with its walls of creamy-gold local stone in which ammonites, some over a foot wide, have been set. These fossils were found in the nearby Portland and Purbeck outcrop from which stone the walls were made. Along the tiny lane we follow is an ornamental well, an Egyptian spring, which helps to fill the lake in the grounds of Hartwell House. The house is associated with the Brett family, of whom one Richard Brett helped to translate the authorised version of the Bible, and was rector of Quainton in 1595. Not only is the house one of splendour but the grounds are a joy to behold. Close by is the rare little eighteenth-century church built to the design of the octagonal chapter house of York Minister.

Moving on and climbing gently by Whaddon Hill Farm, the view ahead is of the quietly flowing river Thame as it skirts around Eythrope Park. In the park we see our first glimpse of the Rothschild five arrows insignia on the house, representing the five sons of one branch of the family. From here the parkland leads to Waddesdon Hill by way of pleasant woodland, and on to Waddesdon itself. The main street is very wide, with many large, red-brick houses also bearing the Rothschild insignia. At one end of the village is the lovely Norman church,

The Egyptian Spring in Weir Lane, Hartwell, on the North Bucks Way (*C. Martland*)

which really does demand a visit. Waddesdon is mainly known for the Manor, now in National Trust care so that we can visit this grand place. The grounds are extensive and beautiful with many secluded corners. An ornamental aviary contains colourful and unusual birds, each having enough room to fly. It was in 1874 that Baron Ferdinand de Rothschild decided to have his home on this Buckinghamshire hillside. The top was made flat, Bath stone was brought up the hill on a specially built steam tramway to create the magnificent structure we see today in the style of a French chateau. Mature trees were hauled up the hill by teams of Percheron mares brought over from France.

Almshouses at Quainton

At Quainton, the North Bucks Way crosses the village green by the stone cross and the tower of Quainton Mill (*C. Martland*)

Then on to Quainton, a village with a sloping green in the middle of which is an old market cross, its octagonal shaft broken, alas. All around the green are quaint cottages, some Tudor, some seventeenth century, and a Queen Anne house. Just down the turning to the church is a row of gabled almshouses with fine chimneys, porches and the heraldic shield of Richard Winwood who built them. Winwood was Deputy Lieutenant of the county in the reign of Charles II. He was also Secretary of State to James I and lived in the manor house of Quainton. Almost adjoining the almshouses is the parish church, fourteenth century with battlements and parapet to its fifteenth-century tower; a fine, lofty building. Simber Hill forms the backdrop to this pleasant corner, with its top uneven as a result of clay extraction. On the lower slope of the hillside is a sail-less tower windmill, 100ft tall and one of the loftiest that functioned in the county. Its bricks were made from the clay on the hill above, one brick at the base dates it at 1830, and when complete it had six floors.

The Way climbs Simber Hill for the view which includes the hills of Muswell, Brill, Waddesdon and Pitchcott. After enjoying this elevation Fulbrook Farm is passed, but not without a glance, for this comfortable complex was built largely with stone plundered from the ruins of the church at Hogshaw, a nearby deserted medieval village. Claydon country is now approached, and all its associations with the Verney family whose four manors are Middle, East, Botolph (or Bottle) and Steeple Claydon. Entering East Claydon on an upward track, we see the tiny church and the seventeenth-century house where lived Sir Arthur Bryant, the eminent historian. This village also has attractive thatched cottages enhanced by carefully tended gardens.

Whilst not on the route, the less visited but very impressive Adam-style Claydon House is close by, and although part is still lived in by the family, the house is in the care of the National Trust. The original house was built at the time of Henry VII but what we see today is middle eighteenth century. The rooms have exquisite ceilings and other rare decorations, and the whispering staircase has sheaths of corn so delicate that a new stairway has been built for daily use. Florence Nightingale spent much time at Claydon and her room shows photographs and writings from her lifetime. The 300 acres of grounds have tall cedars and cypresses grown from seeds brought back by Florence from the Crimean War.

Down hill now to the Verney Arms Hotel with its gay heraldic nameboard, then over the railway line at Verney Junction and across the meadows to Claydon Brook, an important waterway for the draining of many smaller streams and one which can be vicious in flood. When the route was first surveyed, there was no bridge, the old one having disintegrated. All is well now though, and we can cross to the hamlet of Addington easily enough. It was here on a wet Saturday in 1972 that Christopher Hall, then Secretary of the Ramblers' Association, came with a rain-soaked party of ramblers to open the North Bucks Way. Addington consists of a tiny church hidden in trees, the seventeenth-century manor house and a few cottages. In the church is a rare picture of Christ before Pilate, believed to have been painted some 600 years ago. Pleasant open countryside now leads to Great Horwood with its many small Georgian houses overlooked by a fine tower to the church, from which gargoyles stare down with mouths wide open as if mocking passers-by. The church also has fine examples of flowing tracery windows.

The first glimpse of Nash, the next village, is of the pond which completes the dream of a perfect Buckinghamshire village when accompanied by water pump and winding streets of thatched cottages. The pond also brings to mind the Aylesbury Duck, for many of these villages have a pond just for them! Nash and Whaddon were at one time twin parishes, being included in Whaddon Chase where kings once hunted. Alas, as with many ancient woodlands there is little left, but from the plateau on which the church stands, distant views keep the traveller wondering what lies ahead. The church tower is a landmark today, as it has been since the fourteenth century. A peep inside reveals Norman pillars, brasses of exceptional interest and many other items telling of its early days. A row of red almshouses are close by. Just after leaving Whaddon, the imposing Whaddon Hall looks out on to its own lovely parkland and further to the few remaining earthworks of the Benedictine priory of Snelshall.

Two miles ahead, the busy traffic along Roman Watling Street that we prosaically label the A5, will bring us back to reality. We are leaving the peace of Aylesbury Vale behind, but many who have discovered it along this Way will be happy to know that there are many more paths to explore here. Your ideal guide would be the book by local authors Peter and Diana Gulland that describes eighteen more circular walks in the Rothschild and Claydon country, touching on the North Bucks Way and introducing other delights like the witchert villages or the Brill hills. Meanwhile over the A5 the scene changes as we approach Wolverton, built as a railway town with houses for the folk who worked in the carriage shops. It was a thriving town then, where the workers were craftsmen and proud of their calling. Now the town is run by Milton Keynes Development Corporation who are doing their best to make their new city pleasant to live in, and the North Bucks Way follows walkways between the houses.

On reaching the A422 you have two options: to the right is the railway station and services homewards, while ahead a path leads to the Grand Union Canal and further paths into Northamptonshire.

The Grafton and Knightley Ways

It was in 1966 that the East Midlands Area of the Ramblers' Association suggested to Northamptonshire County Council that a series of paths between Badby and Greens Norton should be included in their way-marking programme, to link the youth hostels in the two villages. The council had already begun to waymark selected path routes with their own rather unusual device of a 15in diameter metal disc painted white on both sides, usually mounted on an iron post near to a stile or gate. The ramblers surveyed their route and submitted a list of paths to the county. By early 1972, the paths had all been made walkable, with good stiles and waymarks, and the official opening ceremony could be held at a Ramblers' Association rally at Weedon.

Several names were thought of, but the council's suggestion of Knightley Way finally seemed the most appropriate, as the Knightleys had provided six High Sherriffs of the county between 1698 and 1817, and had for centuries owned much of the countryside through which the new walk passed. So Knightley Way it was, and the Northants footpath officer performed the opening ceremony at the rally. Im-mediately the walk became popular, and soon the idea was put forward of linking it to the North Bucks Way via a further route, to be named Grafton Way because most of the land passed through was owned by the Dukes of Grafton. The Grafton Way was opened in 1975 without formalities. Each walk has its variation on the county waymark—the Grafton Way with a red and white disc, and the Knightley Way with a blue flash on white.

The Grafton Way begins along the towpath of the Grand Union Canal where North Bucks Way walkers will have joined it, a point just a mile from Wolverton Station. For its first full mile the walk is on a high iron aqueduct that carries the canal over the river Great Ouse, the county boundary, here made wider by the waters of the river Tove coming in from the north. Nearby Cosgrove Lock indicates the junction with the now disused Buckingham arm of the canal which finally closed in 1962. Altogether this is a pretty spot with its little cottages and gently moving water on which are many boats, not to mention the ever-hopeful mute swans. Not quite on the route but just a few yards north and worth seeking is bridge No 65, very ornate neo-Gothic with ogival arch and bearing a fine coat of arms, thought to be those of the Dukes of Grafton.

Now something really unusual; the path goes through a low and narrow tunnel with entrances shaped like horseshoes, for this was the means by which the canal horses changed sides with the towing path. We leave the canal now for Cosgrove church, secluded and protected by mature trees. Its fourteenth-century tower has a stately air whilst the thirteenth-century west door beckons the wayfarer to stop awhile. The scene changes as we come to the junction of the A508 and the track to Furtho, where a stop should be made to pick out landmarks. To the west, first Furtho church tower then Potterspury, whilst a little further away is Whittlewood Forest, once one of the royal forests but now much depleted. To the north is the quiet Tove valley with the soaring spire of Hanslope church beyond.

The track continues through Furtho to Potterspury, and although the village is flanked by busy Watling Street it has retained a degree of charm and some thatched cottages. During the enclosure period, boundaries were often defined by drystone walls, but the award for Potterspury and nearby Yardley Gobion in 1775 stipulated quickset hedges with post and rail fences. Such hedges needed additional protection and a frequent direction of the Commissioners was that no lambs or cattle were to be allowed in the fields for a specified period, from four years up to ten, a drastic decision. It is interesting to reflect that many of our lovely may blossom hedges, later in the year aglow with red berries, began as boundaries in the enclosure age. Although much restored, Potterspury church has a long history and being almost in the centre of Grafton country there is much evidence of the family within. The third Duke was Prime Minister in 1767.

A mile further north at Moor End can be seen a good example of ridge and furrow working. This evidence of past land usage is more likely to be found here in the south of the county, as are the signs of medieval villages. The A5 is crossed at the Gullett and then comes a fine stretch of open country leading to Pury End, an especially clean hamlet wherein we might linger to enjoy the cottages of Royal Crescent and a little bridge crossing a bubbling stream on the way out of the

'End'. Another good track leads to Wood Burcot, a one-street hamlet of delightful cottages with colourful gardens wherein its residents doubtless keep a wary eye on nearby growing Towcester to the north. The Way does not go into Towcester but keeps to open country, crossing a tributory of the Tove, and then to the one stretch of hard road on the route, soon covered. At the end of it we are in the water-meadows of the Tove, with the spire of Greens Norton church very evident ahead.

A short, steady climb brings the Way to a housing estate where the last waymark is clearly to be seen. As might be expected, the name Green is associated with the family who held the manor here. One female of the line was the mother of Catherine Parr. The church is surrounded by trees and stands a little higher than the road. Some Saxon remains are in the walls and there are parts of the building from other periods. Tombs to the various Greens are within, showing costume of their day. The graceful spire would be a good subject for the photographer but a forest of wires and posts intrudes. As in other English counties which were divided into sections called Hundreds, in Northamptonshire one was held for Greens Norton. The meetings were held near Field Burcot as it was centrally placed. Doubtless those attending would have been treading the very paths we treasure today.

Before leaving Greens Norton by the blue Knightley Way marker, the opportunity should be taken to look at the Italian-style farmhouses built by a Duke of Grafton, which blend very well with the rest of the village. Our route takes a pleasantly curving path which eventually reveals Caswell, a large house well cared for but no longer a family home because a business organisation now uses it. There is a fine fishpond complete with dam, the stillness of the water complementing the quiet of Caswell itself.

Another isolated farmstead at Foxley is fronted by the ancient drove road called Banbury Lane which runs 22 miles from Banbury where drovers from mid-Wales would join it at the famous Rollright stones in Oxfordshire and follow it to Northampton. The route has become quite isolated now, but in 2 miles it reaches Litchborough with some lovely ironstone buildings which remind us of one of the main livelihoods of the county. Litchborough Hall with its deer park and most impressive gates stands opposite the church and village green. The church is thirteenth century onward, and it seems that the people of Litchborough were well aware of the value of time as there are five scratch dials and a sundial on the tower.

The countryside now becomes much more hilly as Farthingstone is approached. The village presents another delightful picture of warm ironstone buildings, and inside the church are some fine poppyhead pews with humorous carvings much suited to the taste of country folk. Soon after Farthingstone comes a fine track affording easy going and good views. To the north can be seen the village of Everdon on the other side of the valley of a tributary of the river Nene. Near Mantles Heath is appropriately named Knightley Wood. There is an air of expectancy as Preston Capes is approached, for this well-kept village is very picturesque; once there was a religious house of just four monks here. The church stands on the edge of a hill looking towards Fawsley, Arbury Hill and some castellated brick cottages making an interesting contribution to the scene, as does the old castle mound, all that remains of the home of one of William's lords of the manor.

Fawsley now calls for our attention as it was here that the Knightley family lived and left much for today's travellers to find. The medieval church comes first into view, standing on raised ground and partly moated. There is Flemish glass in the windows and Tudor carvings on the pews. Monuments to the Knightleys too, whose occupation of the house dates from 1566 to 1715. The estate is set in some 300 acres. Near the house and church are three lakes which were the necessary fishponds for so isolated a place. Beautiful beech trees frame the buildings, shade the lane and bedeck the hillside. Before the coming of the Knightley family to Fawsley in 1415, there had been tenants living round about, but gradually they were evicted to make way for sheep grazing. The grass-covered mounds around the church are evidence of these earlier settlements.

Fawsley Park climbs up the side of Badby Down, highest point on the Way, and looking back affords a fine view of the hall, church, lakes and the hills beyond. Badby Wood prevents a bird's-eye view of Badby, now quite close, but in spring the sight and smell of the blue-bells more than compensates. The sweeping side of Badby Down affords a gradual descent to this gem of villages. Badby is a double-looped community, each loop a green enclosed by cottages giving protection for livestock in the days when loss could mean disaster for a family. The approach is from the church end of the village, warm with its ironstone cottages and thatch. A most noticeable feature of the church is the clerestory, almost completely made of glass. The manor house was once held by the monastery of Crowland, as were several other places in Northamptonshire.

So ends the journey, not by one but three Ways, deep into the heart of England and its history.

Progressive Mileage	Miles Between	Places on route	Bus service to	Rail Service	Cafes	Accommodation	Inns providing snacks etc	Shops
North Buckinghamshire Way								
		Great Kimble (church)	Aylesbury, Princes Risborough, High Wycombe			●	●	
4½	4½	Bishopstone	—				●	
5¾	1¼	Hartwell	Aylesbury, Thame, Oxford				●	
11¼	5½	Waddesdon	Aylesbury		●	●	●	●
13¼	2	Quainton	Aylesbury				●	
17¾	4½	East Claydon	Oxford, Bicester, Bletchley, Aylesbury					●
19	1¼	Verney Junction	—			●	●	
20	1	Addington	Aylesbury, Buckingham					
22	2	Great Horwood	Stony Stratford				●	
24	2	Nash	as above				●	●
26	2	Whaddon	as above				●	
31½	5½	Wolverton	Northampton, Olney, Newport Pagnell, Bedford	●	●	●	●	●
Grafton Way								
-	-	Wolverton	as above	●	●	●	●	●
1½	1½	Cosgrove	—				●	●
3½	2	Potterspury	Northampton, Stony Stratford	●			●	●
7	3½	Pury End, Paulersbury					●	●
12	5	Greens Norton	Towcester				●	●
Knightley Way								
-	-	Greens Norton	as above				●	●
5½	5½	Litchborough	—				●	●
7	1½	Farthingstone	—				●	
13	6	Badby	Northampton				●	●

There are youth hostels at Greens Norton and Badby, and at Lee Gate 4 miles from Chequers Knap

Early closing: Wednesday afternoon in Bletchley, Thame and Princes Risborough, Thursday in Aylesbury, Greens Norton, Badby, Stony Stratford, Buckingham and Northampton

A Coast to Coast Walk

Geoffrey Berry

Alfred Wainwright's pictorial guides to the Lakeland Fells are known to almost every walker in the Lake District. These little books are as common in pockets and rucksacks as the Ordnance Survey sheets. The seven volumes describe and illustrate the various routes of ascent and descent of all the Lakeland fells, using a technique virtually unique when Wainwright first began his colossal task in 1955. Every detail, every map, every little thumb-nail study and every word of text was in his own hand, drawing an affectionate portrait of the Lakes with a very personal and philosophical touch. He went on to produce, in similar style, other guides which have become universally known, and in particular his *Pennine Way Companion*. Few walkers set out without Wainwright on this first and most famous of long-distance walks.

So it was no wonder that when, in 1973, he offered *A Coast to Coast Walk* as a long-distance route of his own devising, there were many ramblers all ready to set out and try it, with Wainwright's new book grasped in hand. Today, although it remains an 'unofficial' route, it is as well known as any in the land and unique in the way it links east and west coastlines of England. The book describes, with characteristic attention to detail and touches of humour, a walk through splendid country, crossing in its course three National Parks, the Lake District, the Yorkshire Dales and the North York Moors. A third of the total distance of 190 miles falls within these three parks. A journey on foot from the Irish Sea to the North Sea has its own fascination, and it is with a sense of adventure that we set out from the promenade at St Bees to climb the path above red sandstone cliffs. As we turn eastwards from the headland, it is to be hoped that the enthusiasm of that first morning will enable us to ignore the proximity of the huge chemical works and the southern outskirts of Whitehaven.

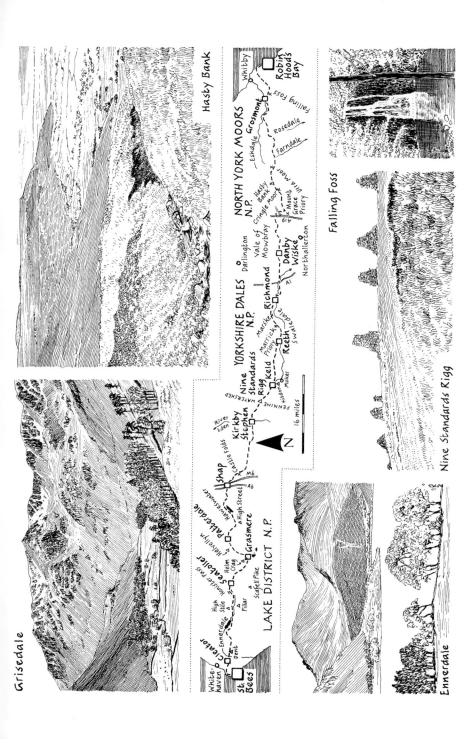

Grisedale

Hasty Bank

NORTH YORK MOORS N.P.

Whitby

Robin Hood's Bay

Falling Foss

Eskdale Grosmont

Rosedale

Farndale

Vale of Cringle Moors

Darlington Mowbray Hasty Bank

Ilam Moor

Mount Grace Priory

A19

Danby Wiske

Northallerton

A1

YORKSHIRE DALES N.P.

Richmond

Marske

Matricky Priory

Reeth

Swaledale

Keld Muker

Nine Standards Rigg Kisdon

Rigg

PENNINE WATERSHED

River Eden

Kirkby Stephen

Shap

Castle Folds

16 miles

N

Haweswater

M6

A6

High Street

LAKE DISTRICT N.P.

Patterdale

Grasmere

Helvellyn

Helm Crag

Seatoller

Honister Pass

Scafell Pike

High Stile

Pillar

Ennerdale Stile

Ennerdale Dent

White Haven

St. Bees

Falling Foss

Nine Standards Rigg

Ennerdale

It is beyond Cleator, on the path which ascends the eminence called Dent (1131ft), that the expedition really starts. Ahead of us are mountains and moorlands, lakes and dales, heather paths and green tracks. After a few miles of easy walking we reach the shore of Ennerdale Water at its outflow into the river Ehen. The path, now in places rough and stony, runs at the foot of the bilberry-clothed fellside until it reaches the steep rock of Anglers' Crag which drops directly into the lake. The traverse across the face of the Crag is not difficult, involving only a little clambering over rocks and scree, but this may be avoided by taking the higher route over the top of the Crag, with magnificent views of Ennerdale. Across the waters of the lake and matching the bastion on which we stand, is rocky Bowness Knott guarding the entrance to the valley. Beyond runs the ridge of Red Pike and High Stile dividing Ennerdale from Buttermere. Up the valley, rising above the carpet of forest, is Pillar mountain dominant in the scene, its northern slopes broken by the outline of Pillar Rock.

Before we go on we should perhaps glance momentarily behind us at the seemingly flat coastal plain and at the sweep of industrial West Cumbria which we are leaving for higher, simpler and more lovely things. The path along the shore of Ennerdale Water through the natural woodland of scattered ash, oak, and birch, is one with a strong feeling of escape and where the hand of man is little evident. Rights of way encircle the lake and make possible a pleasant excursion of some 6 miles from the parking places at Bowness Point or at the western end of the lake.

Our route on to the head of Ennerdale crosses the bright and pure water of the river Liza by footbridge, and continues by forest road to the remote and lonely Black Sail Hostel, where we may well spend the night. The afforestation of the floor of Ennerdale gave rise to a great deal of criticism in the 1930s, when it was rightly contended that the regimented ranks of conifers and their straight boundaries would damage the dramatic bareness of the mountains. The objections led to an agreement in 1936 between the CPRE and the Forestry Commission that no further planting would take place in the central 300 square miles of the Lake District. The agreement is still in force.

Walkers on the path near Anglers' Crag, Ennerdale (*Geoffrey Berry*)

Out of Ennerdale into Borrowdale

The way climbs out of Ennerdale, now well beyond the forest, to almost 2000ft beside Loft Beck, and continues at this height with Brandreth and Grey Knotts rising to our right. As we descend to the Honister, there is ample evidence of green-slate quarrying which has gone on here since the seventeenth century. There are new workings high on the slopes of Fleetwith Pike, and when we reach the pass we can see, far out on the precipices of Honister Crag, the remains of ancient workings now only to be reached by perilous tracks. Over the top we make a long, easy descent by the old green-turfed toll road to Seatoller, where there is a good cafe and accommodation if needs be.

Now for a few miles we are walking in the heart of Borrowdale. We go through Johnny's Wood, indigenous oak woodland scheduled as of Special Scientific Interest, and on beside the river Derwent to the little hamlet of Rosthwaite. There we turn up the Stonethwaite Beck and climb out of Borrowdale by Greenup Gill; its tumbling waters sing and its clear pools show the varied colours of the smooth boulders of volcanic rock. From Greenup Edge, the summit of the pass, there is, in clear weather, a glimpse of Grasmere to give us our direction, for the descent into Far Easedale is not the most obvious but across the head of numerous tributaries of the Wyth Burn. Wainwright's preferred route is along the ridge of Calf Crag and Gibson Knott to the summit of Helm Crag (the Lion and the Lamb). Here the huge, strangely shaped and tumbled rocks repay an hour's exploration and the many crevasses provide sheltered places even on wild days. We may sit and watch with god-like detachment traffic crawling far below on Dunmail Raise, before the steep drop into Grasmere. The village has many associations with Wordsworth—nearby is the cottage where he lived, and in the churchyard is his grave.

Grisedale, with the Helvellyn range beyond. The Coast to Coast Walk curves down the valley (*Geoffrey Berry*)

From Grasmere we are faced with the long climb to Grisedale Pass, but then again there is a long, steady and pleasant descent, first touching the shore of Grisedale Tarn and then by Ruthwaite Lodge and Grisedale Beck to Patterdale. More spectacular routes may be taken from Grisedale Tarn, either swinging north by Dollywaggon Pike, Helvellyn summit and Striding Edge, or eastwards by Deepdale Hause and St Sunday Crag. The second course is much less travelled and it gives dramatic views of the eastern corries of the Helvellyn range.

The Helvellyn Range from Angle Tarn

Patterdale to Haweswater's shores

From Patterdale to the eastern boundaries of the Lake District, we must pass over the mountain range of High Street and climb to at least 2500ft. It is a splendid walk by an almost continuously rising path which twists and turns among the hills after an initial ascent across the lower slopes of Place Fell to Boardale Hause. The views in all directions are of a mountainous countryside with delightfully wooded valleys.

The southern reach of that most beautiful of lakes, Ullswater, stretches behind us, and ahead on the skyline is the curve of Kirkstone Pass and its enclosing mountains. Beyond a narrow defile above Boardale Hause, the path emerges on an elevated terrace before it swings eastwards and, skirting Angletarn Pikes, drops to the Tarn, caught in its secluded hollow. This is a place to linger if there is time and the day is good. In warm sunshine the shore and islands are irresistibly inviting, and there is a sense of peace and remoteness from all the cares of civilisation. The path goes on by Satura Crag, curves around The Knott, crosses the Roman road on High Street, still discernible in its rutted course along the ridge, climbs the shoulder of Rampsgill Head and commences on the long descent to the shores of Haweswater. The hard work is done; we climb again only a little way, now borne on by our momentum, to take in the summit of Kidsty Pike (2560ft), a fine viewpoint standing prominently above the remote and unpopulated valley of Riggindale.

The Coast to Coast Path along the shores of Haweswater, after a light fall of snow
(*Geoffrey Berry*)

We reach the shore of Haweswater near the ruins of Riggindale Farm. This valley was flooded and depopulated by Manchester Corporation in the 1930s when their second reservoir in the Lake District was constructed here. Much of the wild beauty remains, but at times when the water level is drawn down, there is an air of devastation and sterility over the dale. The only inhabited building above the dam is the Haweswater Hotel on the far side of the lake, which provides good accommodation. Our path, running northwards close to the shore, is a pleasant one, well trodden and undemanding, quiet and far away from traffic. The hills run up on our left hand, sometimes steep and craggy and sometimes into great lonely corries which invite exploration. On the summit of Birks Crag soon after we join the lakeside path, there are remains of an early British fort, a tiny elevated place which must have been the home of some small tribe in this wild, hostile countryside. They did not look down on these extensive waters but on a smaller lake which occupied the lower reaches of Mardale before the flooding. Becks of varying capacities bring tumbling waters down from the hills, the largest being the Measand Beck which drops down the steep and rocky escarpment above the path. It is well worth climbing to the head of the falls, going upstream for a few hundred yards to a bridge and then descending on the far side for a proper appreciation of Measand Force. However, if our energies are flagging, there is a bridge on the path crossing the beck below the falls. A little further on, there is a glimpse of the concrete dam through the belt of spruce which here borders the reservoir, and then we go down to Burn Banks.

We are now entering a quite different landscape of fields, farmland and scattered trees in the valley of the river Lowther. The wild and uninhabited country and the high mountains are behind us; there are gates and stiles, fences and cattle, but it remains a quiet and unspoiled scene. The path reaches the river Lowther at Rosgill Bridge, where we do not cross but go upstream to a lovely pack-horse bridge which spans Swindale Beck, a tributary of the Lowther. This little bridge, well off modern routes, must have been used for centuries by people going to Shap Abbey, the ruins of which are less than a mile ahead. The Abbey, built in the twelfth and thirteenth centuries, was placed on the narrow floor of this steep-sided valley, and its still substantial tower rises level with the crest of the valley sides. It is a secluded, sheltered spot where we might put down our rucksacks and wander among the fashioned stones and truncated pillars, before the gentle climb and road walk into Shap.

Shap is a long drawn out place, high and windswept, and since the opening of the M6, reasonably peaceful, freed from the continuous thunder of heavy vehicles. Shap village has for centuries lain across one of the main routes into Scotland and in consequence many of its buildings are in early vernacular architecture. It is interesting to wander about the lanes which run parallel to the main road and on the numerous stiled footpaths which radiate through the maze of limestone walls to such places as the Goggleby Stone, a monolith which was part, it is thought, of a huge prehistoric monument.

Upland limestone

We are now on the upland limestone, a terrain which has always appealed to man. It is well drained and provides good turf and productive soil. It was in such country as this that Stone-Age man dwelt, and here is much evidence of his early activities. There are stone circles, standing stones and tumuli, and we pass close to some of them. Limestone is today sought after by man in devastating ways, and we see evidence of this all too clearly in the works and extensive quarries near Shap village. Nor is this the only distraction of modern civilisation we have temporarily to endure. As soon as we leave Shap the noise of traffic on the M6 impinges, and it remains with us for 3 or 4 miles. We cross the roaring highway on an elevated single beam of concrete, one of only three footbridges over the M6 in Cumbria. It is strange then, that a second and similar bridge is in sight less than a mile to the north. Almost immediately we face a huge limestone quarry and, although its negotiation is provided for by stiles and wooden steps, it is important to find the exact route. We are now close to Oddendale, a remote cluster of farms and agricultural buildings in the shelter of a wide belt of tall trees. As we turn southwards on a track running over short limestone turf, we have about us a panorama stretching from the Lakeland peaks to the Pennine range. In spring, the call of lapwing and the song of the skylark replaces the noise of traffic and the clatter of quarry machinery.

For the 16 miles to Kirkby Stephen, it is a countryside largely unaltered through the centuries, but there is much of interest on the moorland. Here are the scattered, glacier-borne boulders of Shap granite, a distinctive pinkish rock containing quantities of large felspar crystals. Some of the boulders are huge and rounded, lying where they were deposited at the end of the last ice age. Some were gathered by ancient man 3,000 years ago to build stone circles. There is a good example close to our track south-west of Oddendale, with two concentric circles and an internal cairn. On the opposite side of the track about half a mile away are the remains of another burial cairn. On these stretches of high moorland, once the home of our ancestors, we are unlikely now to see anyone. We curve around the head waters of the Lyvennet Beck running north into the delightful valley which contains Crosby Ravensworth and Maulds Meaburn. The limestone has been overlain by acid soils which carry wide expanses of heather. Here in this lonely place, the army of Charles II rested to drink the clear water of Black Dub, the source of the Lyvennet, and we might well do the same. A monument marks the spot.

The strange limestone pavement on Great Asby Scar. The highest ground is Castle Folds, an early British settlement which the walk passes (*Geoffrey Berry*)

Across the unfenced Kendal to Appleby road we climb low scars on to the exposed sheets of water-worn limestone, with its strange formations and deep fissures. These limestone pavement areas are a dramatic and infrequent phenomenon and a rich habitat for flora. We come to a very fine example on Great Asby Scar where there are beds of limestone in varying surface formations, from huge slabs divided by deep fern-filled grykes, to small flaky masses of rock set in herb-rich turf. In this area of exposed limestone there is a strange, circular, projecting rocky platform upon which the early Britons established a camp, Castle Folds. There are remains of walls, cairns and hut circles within this forbidding site. We take the gentle decline to Sunbiggin Tarn, a reedy place, the haunt of wildfowl and in particular the noisily declared home of thousands of black-headed gulls. The road verges hereabouts are colourful in June with that delicate, lovely and generally rare flower, the bird's-eye primrose (*primula farinosa*). Our route eastwards takes us by more prehistoric remains, Rayseat Pike long barrow and Severals village settlement, then down across the Scandal Beck on ancient Smardale bridge, and on to a wide, green track. This must once have been the coach road to Kirkby Stephen, now long abandoned except by people such as ourselves. It is a pleasant walk in the moorland scented air of late afternoon, with the great outlines of Wild Boar Fell and Mallerstang to the south and the Eden valley and the Pennines ahead, into the hospitable little town of Kirkby Stephen. It can well supply all our simple needs.

Over the Pennine watershed

Leaving Kirkby Stephen, we have before us the crossing of the Pennines. The climb is a steady one by Hartley village and then by an old cart track, well engineered, to former coal pits at over 2000ft. From here it is less than a mile to the summit of Nine Standards Rigg (2171ft); the going is peat-boggy and typically Pennine. It is said that the nine cairns were built to give the marauding Scots the impression that an English army was encamped here. On the Rigg in poor weather, there seems to be nothing but a waste about us, identical in every direction. For our onward journey though, once we have located the head waters of the Whitsundale Beck, or in better weather taken the watershed to Coldbergh Edge, our navigational difficulties should be over for many miles to come. We are soon in the Yorkshire Dales National Park above the infant Swale and in the healthy roar of its rapids and waterfalls. The tiny hamlet of Keld is at hand, and we may well consider staying at its youth hostel.

Wainwright's preferred route from Keld is almost directly eastwards across the moorland on old miners' tracks linking the abandoned lead workings. He acknowledges the beauty of the riverside paths which are almost continuous from Keld to Reeth, but chooses the higher ground to the north of the valley, crossing the tongues of moorland between the deep incisions cut by the Swale's tributaries. The isolated hill of Kisdon (1636ft) bounded on its north and east by the Swale, and by a tributary and the road on its other sides, is a particularly attractive place which may be encircled on foot or ascended by a bridleway from Muker to Keld, as additional excursions. To pursue our expedition, the preferred route crosses Gunnerside Gill and descends to the main valley by a lengthy track alongside Hard Level Gill to Surrender Bridge. Many old lead-mining buildings are passed and there is much evidence of former workings. Shafts and levels mark the hillside and gullies, and spoil heaps remain stark and barren. The mines came into production in the seventeenth and eighteenth centuries, but the industry collapsed rapidly towards the end of the nineteenth century in the face of cheap foreign imports. Something of the past activity in these now lonely hills can be imagined by a contemplation of the buildings and works at Blakethwaite and Old Gang, both of which we pass. From Surrender Bridge we are at the edge of the valley pastures until we descend into Reeth.

Reeth Onwards

It is an easy ramble from Reeth to Richmond, a distance of 10 miles or so but one with its own delights. We go by Marrick Priory which, established in the twelfth century, was the home of the Benedictine order until the Dissolution. In recent years there has been some restoration, and new buildings have been added for its use as an outdoor

Richmond from over the Swale. The path now follows the near bank of the river downstream (*Geoffrey Berry*)

pursuits centre. We take the charming flagged path upwards through the woods to Marrick, and then on across fields with stiled walls to join the road through the village of Marske, spaciously set out in an undulating wooded countryside. From here into Richmond, there are wide views across the valley of the adult Swale as we walk below cliffs of limestone on the northern slopes and into Whitcliffe Wood.

Richmond is a pleasant town with its central cobbled market place, its noble castle, its numerous alleyways and riverside paths. There are walks on the steep river banks below the castle walls and twisting medieval ginnels to explore, where secluded cottages cling to the rocky hillside and the motor car cannot penetrate. If there is a day to spare on our journey we could spend it here. For an evening stroll, one could take the riverside path to Easby Abbey and return by the disused railway line, now converted to a footpath by the district council. There are also riverside paths upstream which could be followed with a return by bus; Richmond is well served by buses. It is understandable if we leave this unique little town with some reluctance, for we have before us the 22 miles to Ingleby Cross, the least interesting part of our journey.

The first few miles are tolerable enough as we wander through woodland and fields close to the south bank of the Swale. Disillusionment comes with the roar of the traffic on the A1; close beyond is the worldliness of Catterick Bridge, and then the devastation of extensive sand and gravel workings. But soon our environs improve, the tiny hamlet of Bolton-on-Swale has some attraction and perhaps there is consolation to be found in the Jenkins' Memorial in the village churchyard. Jenkins died in the year 1670, aged 169. It does not record whether he was a keen walker. A mile further on, having crossed a number of fields, we strike the tarmac again. The road is, however, quiet and pleasant, slightly undulating, passing through plantations, bounded by grass verges and low hawthorn hedges set with mature trees. The road twists and turns and there is little traffic. We can tramp along without thinking about route finding, hopefully content under a spacious sky. As we progress, the North Yorkshire Moors become more clear ahead and we look forward to their slopes and contours. Beyond the crossing of the A167, we can take a variety of paths, tracks and lanes to Ingleby Cross, our road walking, at least in any stretch over a mile, done with for a long way to come.

On to the North Yorkshire Moors

At Ingleby Cross, we enter our third National Park, the North York Moors. If we have made a forced march from Richmond, we shall almost certainly be in need of a night's rest, and it is as well to book a bed in advance at the Blue Bell Inn, Ingleby Cross.

The western escarpment of the moor is ahead, and from Arncliffe Hall we take a rising track through the woodland to the summit of Beacon Hill (982ft). This is a good viewpoint to be especially appreciated after our traverse of the lower country. Southwards is the Vale of York, westwards the Vale of Mowbray and in the distance the long line of Pennines with the conspicuous indentation of Swaledale. Northwards are the Durham moors seen across the Cleveland Plain and Teesside. This latter view will remain with us as we walk eastwards along, or near to, the edge of the Cleveland escarpment. It is from the Ordnance Survey column on Beacon Hill that the Lyke Wake Walk starts, a journey of 40 miles overlapping our own for some 10 miles. The more energetic contend that this crossing of the moors should be completed in 24 hours, and many succeed in doing so. On Beacon Hill we also pick up the Cleveland Way, an 'official' long-distance footpath, and follow it to beyond Urra Moor. This coincidence of paths is an indication of the attractiveness to walkers of this elevated, although undulating, route.

The best of all times to cross the North Yorkshire Moors is when the heather is in bloom. It is sad that it is only at its peak so briefly, about two weeks in mid-August, the precise time and duration being dependent on weather conditions. In its full glory the heather, stretching deep purple to the horizon, is an unforgettable sight. At close quarters the flowers are of various shades from deep colours to paler and more delicate tints, but in the vast expanse the moors are painted uniformly with a splendid richness. Our boots become dusted with the golden pollen and the air has a scent which seems to bear the very essence of romantic travel in wild and lonely places. To walk on the moors at this time, if but for a day in a lifetime, is an experience not to be missed.

From Beacon Hill we drop down over the open moor to Scarth Nick, cross Scugdale and then climb on to Live Moor to follow the undulating watershed by Carlton Bank, Cringle Moor, Cold Moor and Hasty Bank to the Stokesley–Helmsley road at Clay Bank Top. Cringle Moor, crowned by a tumulus and the second highest summit on the Cleveland hills (1427ft), is worth a visit, even though our path, now well worn, runs along the edge of the craggy northern escarpment. On Hasty Bank there are the Wainstones, a great pile of rocks where shelter is to be found whichever way the wind is blowing.

From Clay Bank Top, we climb on to the great flat-topped heather-covered expanse of Urra Moor, although even here man has left evidence of his activities in guide and boundary stones, tumuli, ordnance columns, modern notices, and the working of iron ore. We pick up the grassy track of the former Rosedale ironstone railway, which contours around the head of Farndale and takes us over High Blakey

The path on the steep wooded slopes near Falling Foss, in the North Yorkshire Moors National Park (*Geoffrey Berry*)

Moor almost to the Lion Inn. There is more heather moorland, Danby High and Glaisdale Moors, before we descend into wooded, steep-sided and charming Eskdale. The miles beside the river to Grosmont bring another dimension to our journey, a contrast to the desolate moorland over which we have just tramped. There are new and more intimate features in the more limited world about us such as the delect-able path, paved in the distant past, through East Arncliffe Wood. We pass through the village of Grosmont set upon its steep hill and cross over Sleights Moor, with its ancient standing stones, into the valley of the Littlebeck. Here again is a lovely path through woodland, fresh and perfumed in early spring, laid with a colourful carpet of fallen leaves in autumn, delightful at any time of the year and enjoyable in any weather. There are beeches high above the beck on the steep sides above Falling Foss; the fall's delicate curtain drops into a deep, dark pool. The path winds on close beside the May Beck to climb eventually on to Sneaton Low Moor and across thick heather, here with little sign of use, to the Whitby–Scarborough road.

In the final stages, Wainwright advises against a direct march on Robin Hood's Bay and recommends a 5 mile detour to the north by Hawsker to finish by a walk along the edge of the cliffs. This is well worthwhile. For an hour or more we have the wide expanse of the North Sea on our left and time to contemplate, in the strong salt air, the varied miles over which we have tramped. As we descend the steep, narrow streets of Robin Hood's Bay itself and pass between its jumbled ancient houses we taste the satisfaction of achievement and feel the insistent call of new expeditions.

A Coast to Coast Walk

Progressive Mileage	Miles Between	Places on route	Bus service to	Rail Service	Cafes	Accommodation	Inns providing snacks etc	Shops	Camping
-	-	St. Bees	Whitehaven	●	●	●	●	●	
9	9	Cleator	Whitehaven, Egremont			●	●	●	Black How Farm
14	5	Ennerdale Bridge	Whitehaven		●	●	●		
29	15	Rosthwaite	Keswick		●	●	●	●	Chapel Farm
38	9	Grasmere	Keswick, Kendal	●	●	●	●		
47	9	Patterdale	Penrith, Windermere		●	●	●	●	Side Farm, Patterdale
63	16	Shap	Penrith, Kendal	●	●	●	●		
83	20	Kirkby Stephen	Penrith, Appleby	●	●	●	●		
96	13	Keld	Richmond				●		
107	11	Reeth	Richmond	●	●	●	●		
117	10	Richmond	Darlington, Northallerton, Keld, Leyburn, Hawes	●	●	●		●	Thornborough Farm (A1)
131	14	Danby Wiske	—				●	●	The Green, Danby Wiske
140	9	Ingleby Cross	Teeside, Thirske, Northallerton			●	●	●	
152	12	Clay Bank Top	Teeside, Helmsley		●				
171	19	Glaisdale	—		●		●	●	●
174	3	Grosmont	—		●	●	●	●	●
185	11	Hawsker	Scarborough, Whitby			●	●	●	●	York House, High Hawsker
190	5	Robin Hood's Bay	Scarborough, Whitby			●	●	●	●

There are youth hostels at Gillerthwaite and Black Sail (Ennerdale), Honister Pass, Rosthwaite, Grasmere, Patterdale, Kirkby Stephen, Keld, Grinton Lodge, Westerdale, Boggle Hole, (Robin Hood's Bay)

Early closing: Wednesday afternoon in St. Bees and Richmond. Thursday in Grasmere, Shap, Kirkby Stephen and Reeth

Camping: there are numerous unofficial sites on the high fells, moors and common land crossed by the route

The Cotswold Way

Tony Drake

The 100 mile Cotswold Way can claim to provide one of Britain's most scenic week-long walks. By following mostly along the top of the steep western escarpment of the Cotswold Hills, it has many of the characteristics of a coast path except that one has the varied expanse of the Severn Vale and distant hills spread before you instead of the sea.

This is a walk that sustains its scenic qualities throughout. It is never dull, but a succession of changing landscapes of green fields and trees of the most pleasing kind. Not only is the landscape a softer one than, say, the chalk downs of the Ridgeway Path, but the villages are gems of stone in the mellow local limestone. Time should be allowed to walk slowly round the villages and small towns on the route. Only when crossing the Stroud valley at Ryeford will you be conscious of passing through a semi-industrial area.

The Cotswold Hills form the central part of a belt of limestone that crosses England from the Dorset coast in the south to Lincolnshire. The lie of the Cotswold limestone is such that it slopes away towards the east, but has been eroded on its western side to form a sharp drop into the Severn Vale. Intersecting valleys and some outlying hills near to the main escarpment all contribute to the fascinating scenery. The Cotswold Way weaves its course, mostly along the top of the escarpment but sometimes along the western side where there are interesting places to visit just off the hills. Its highest point is on Cleeve Common at just over 1000ft, most other parts of the escarpment being over 700ft.

The long history

When the National Parks Act went on the statute book in December 1949, it provided for a first-ever survey of rights of way, and of course for the establishment of long-distance paths. Just a month before, I had become secretary of the Gloucestershire committee of the Ramblers' Association, so my first task was to organise our efforts to see that all rights of way were recorded under the coming survey. At the same time, we began to consider whether any long-distance paths should be created in or through the county. A route along the Cotswold escarpment seemed an obvious choice, but there was no encouragement from the report of the Hobhouse Committee which preceded the National Parks Act. Of the routes they proposed, only Offa's Dyke would touch Gloucestershire.

Despite this a route along the Cotswold edge was planned, including several sections which would require new rights of way to be created. There were also several sections where the right of way status was in doubt, and these received our priority attention. At seven points along the present route within Gloucestershire, the path is on the definitive map because we claimed it back in the early 1950s. By 1953, when some of the pressure of this claiming process had lessened, our committee finalised its proposals for a Cotswold Way and sent them to the National Parks Commission. It gained an encouraging reference in the Commission's 1953 annual report, but by then they had many routes in the making and little more was heard of it.

In 1968, the Gloucestershire Planning Department carried out a recreational survey which prominently featured the Cotswold Way as a future long-distance footpath. We were pleased, but a little taken aback, when the county council told us they intended to open the route during the national footpath week we were planning for 1970. The whole walk was to be on existing public ways, including many miles on roads. We feared, rightly as it transpired, that such hasty designation might prejudice its ultimate recognition as an official long-distance path, but nevertheless we gave Ramblers' Association support to the idea and arranged for nine local rambling clubs to walk the whole route between them on the opening day, 17 May 1970.

The Cotswold Way received the first year's allocation of funds for path signposting when Gloucestershire was forced by the Countryside Act of 1968 to spend money on such amenities. Then, in 1975, a programme of complete waymarking was begun, many path problems were overcome, and the efforts of voluntary wardens of the Cotswold

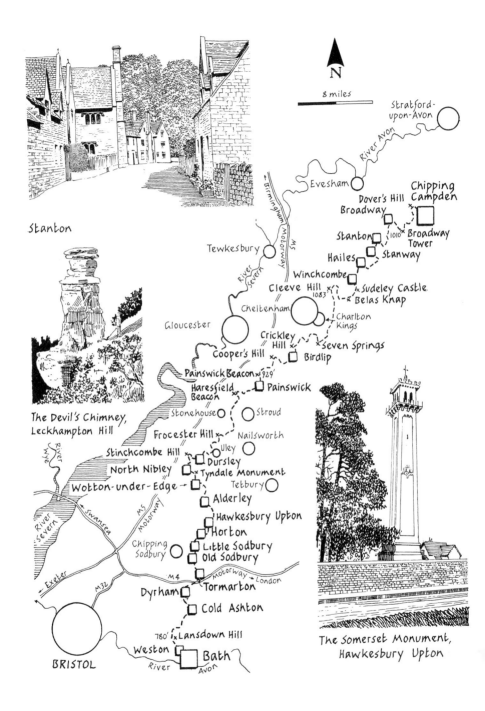

N

8 miles

Stratford-upon-Avon

River Avon

Evesham

Dover's Hill

Broadway

Chipping Campden

Stanton

Birmingham Motorway M5

Tewkesbury

Stanton 1010 Broadway Tower

Hailes Stanway

Winchcombe

River Severn

Cleeve Hill 1083 Sudeley Castle

Belas Knap

Cheltenham

Charlton Kings

Gloucester

Crickley Hill

Seven Springs

Cooper's Hill Birdlip

Painswick Beacon 929

Haresfield Beacon

Painswick

The Devil's Chimney, Leckhampton Hill

Stonehouse Stroud

Frocester Hill Nailsworth

River Wye

Stinchcombe Hill Uley

Dursley

North Nibley Tyndale Monument

Wotton-under-Edge Tetbury

Alderley

Hawkesbury Upton

Horton

River Severn

Swansea

M5 Motorway

Chipping Sodbury

Little Sodbury

Old Sodbury

Exeter

M4

Motorway London

M32

Tormarton

Dyrham

Cold Ashton

780 Lansdown Hill

Weston

BRISTOL

Bath

River Avon

The Somerset Monument, Hawkesbury Upton

Warden Service have brought improvements to many sections. But alas, the Cotswold Way is unlikely now to join the list of official long-distance paths, despite its worthiness for such designation. No doubt today's Countryside Commission would cover half the cost of needed improvements under its 'Footpaths for Recreation' scheme, but still Gloucestershire, together with the other counties involved, Avon and Herefordshire/Worcestershire, would need to find the other half. Meanwhile the main deficiency of the Cotswold Way remains—the absence of new paths to replace road sections.

Finding your way

The Cotswold Way is easier to follow than most long-distance routes. This is due partly to the splendid guide book by Mark Richards, but also to the high standard of signposting and waymarking. This is claimed to be the most comprehensive and effective of any of the long-distance routes in Britain, of whatever status. The waymarking system used is based on that recommended by the Countryside Commission.

Arrows are painted on gates, stiles, trees, walls, uprights of signposts, etc., and always placed to face the oncoming walker. An arrow pointing straight up means straight on, and a tilt to one side indicates a corresponding change of direction. The colour of the arrows depends on the status of the highway at that point—footpaths are marked in yellow and bridleways in blue. White arrows are also used where the route is along a road, although this is not part of the Countryside Commission scheme. By each arrow is a white spot about the size of an old penny, to identify the Cotswold Way. The reason for this extra symbol is that the arrow system is intended for all paths, and although most paths to either side of the Cotswold Way are not waymarked yet, they may be in the future.

The waymark arrows have been placed to be read in whichever direction you are walking the Way. Difficult junctions are sometimes marked with a 'headless arrow' technique. The junction arrow has straight stems for each possible way, but only the Cotswold Way has an arrowhead on the stem. Where it is difficult to see the path across a large field, a white disc will sometimes guide you, similar to the type used on golf courses when the hole cannot be seen from the tee. In towns the waymarking, particularly useful in finding the way through a housing estate, is usually put on the upright part of kerbstones.

Although there are voluntary inspectors who maintain the waymarks, all manner of happenings can break the continuity of the waymarking chain. If you find any missing or misleading waymarks on the Cotswold Way, please report them to the Ramblers' Association or to the Head Warden, Cotswolds AONB, Shire Hall, Gloucester.

A word about maps. Although the waymarking is so fine, and the Cotswold Way is also signposted wherever it leaves roads, we strongly recommend that you carry maps. But here you will find that the new 1:50 000 scale OS maps do not cover the route nearly as conveniently as the old 1in series. You need five sheets of the new series against two sheets of the old—18oz to carry as against 4oz. Such is progress!

Because of the slow appearance of the 2nd series 1:25 000 OS maps (only two are available which cover part of the Way), the Ramblers' Association in Gloucestershire have obtained Ordnance Survey permission to produce special composite three-colour maps covering the country traversed by the Cotswold Way. All public highways are marked, either in green for paths and untarred roads, or in orange for tarred roads. Commons are shaded in green, and the Cotswold Way prominently marked with periodic orange spots. So far only two of the proposed series of six sheets have been published, but the standard of production is high enough to compete with OS maps and they insist on a selling price comparable with their equivalent maps.

From Chipping Campden to Bath

The wool-market hall at Chipping Campden seems the obvious northern terminus of the Cotswold Way. This beautiful old building in Cotswold stone, mercifully preserved by the National Trust, stands half way along the gently curving main street of Campden, a street flanked by gems of Cotswold architecture that make it one of the

Starting point of the Cotswold Way, looking out from the market hall of Chipping Campden (*Leonard and Marjorie Gayton*)

famous streets of the world. Some would have the Cotswold Way
start at the church and pass by the almshouses and Grevel's house.
These must certainly be visited, but it is more logical for the Way to
start in the middle of the little town.

The route leaves the main street and ascends Hoo Lane to Dover's
Hill. Here is the first of the many views that the Cotswold Way walker
sees across the Severn Vale. The slopes form a natural amphitheatre
which was the scene of the 'Olympic Games' started by Robert Dover
and which ran for a couple of centuries until the coming of the railways,
when mobs from the Midlands led to their discontinuance. In those
days there were events such as cock fighting and shin kicking,
but these form no part of the revived games which take place each
spring.

The Lygon Arms, Broadway

At Stanway the Cotswold Way passes by the fine Inigo Jones gatehouse to the Hall
(*Leonard and Marjorie Gayton*)

After leaving the National Trust topograph, a short road walk leads past the Kiftsgate Stone to the Mile Drive, a long field over which the public right of way was only firmly established after a day and a half of wrangling at quarter sessions in 1966. Soon we begin the climb to Broadway Tower, a folly built to be seen from miles around. It can be ascended, and is now part of a Country Park with a cafe and nature trails.

Now comes the first of several descents into the Vale. The reason is the fabulous main street of Broadway, in which fine Cotswold houses have been preserved, many as antique shops or cafes. Of particular note is the four-star Lygon Arms Hotel, of world renown, with the associated Gordon Russell furniture enterprise tucked away behind.

From Broadway, the Way gently climbs up to Burhill and back into Gloucestershire after its 3 mile incursion into Worcestershire. Tracks are followed with fine views on the right to No Man's Land whence the second descent to the Vale is made. This time the justification comes in the twin villages of Stanton and Stanway. The former is a

The Cotswold Way follows the main street of Stanton, a perfect Cotswold village
(*British Tourist Authority*)

model Cotswold village and Stanway is noted for the palatial gatehouse
to Stanway House by Inigo Jones. The route returns to the upper level
at Stumps Cross and follows the ancient Campden Lane to Cromwell's
Clump, a viewpoint from which Thomas Cromwell is said to have
watched the burning of Hailes Abbey.

Hailes Abbey was for three centuries a place of great pilgrimage to
see an alleged sample of the blood of Christ, but a few arches and walls
are all that now remain above the ground. The setting is attractive,
however, and the remains, together with the museum, are worth a visit
(they are not open on Sunday mornings).

The Pilgrim's Way from Hailes to Winchcombe is probably the
most historic route followed by the Cotswold Way, though apart
from a few stones which formed part of its paving, there is little to

suggest that this was once an important highway between abbeys. It is a waymarker's nightmare, as there are humps in several fields which obscure the point of exit, some unnatural bends in the path, and obvious gates are not always the correct way out. To help, the arrow way-marking is being supplemented with tall posts and white discs.

Winchcombe, once an important town of Mercian England with an abbey, now completely vanished, has much to offer with interesting inns like the George, the church's gargoyles, and nearby Sudeley Castle, high in the stately homes' attendance list. The Way between Winchcombe and Cleeve Hill makes a wide detour south to include the important archaeological site of Belas Knap, a stone-age long barrow. The path from Winchcombe weaves its way up to this well-preserved tumulus, then makes for Cleeve Common. The common is large and the nearest approach to open moorland in Gloucestershire. On its eastern side there is a real feeling of remoteness, while on its craggy western side, the spa town of Cheltenham is spread before you.

From the Cotswold Way on Cleeve Hill, the views are to the distant Malvern and Clee Hills (*Leonard and Marjorie Gayton*)

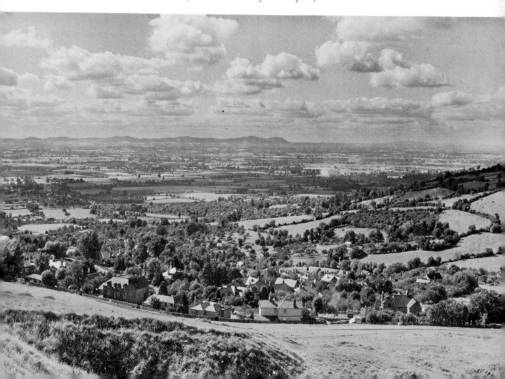

The focal point is Cleeve Cloud with its trig point and topograph, although at 1040ft this is not the highest point of the common. A quick descent brings you to Cleeve Hill youth hostel, the only one right by the Cotswold Way.

For 5 miles the western flank of the Cleeve plateau is followed south to the busy A40 Cheltenham–London road, near the beautiful tree-lined Dowdeswell reservoir. The Way then winds up through fields and woods to emerge on Ravensgate Hill, where a narrow path gradually ascends what must be one of the steepest parts of the Cotswold escarpment. Alas, there follows a diabolical mile of the A436 road, shortly to be made wider and faster. You could make a wide detour via Upper Coberley, but this is a case where a new right of way is particularly needed, and one would certainly have been created by now if this route had been officially recognised.

A short diversion to Seven Springs is rewarded with the picturesque sight of what many consider to be the source of the Thames. Certainly the Churn is a longer and higher rising tributary than the official source near Cirencester. Return is made to the escarpment at Leckhampton Hill with its grotesque pillar of Devil's Chimney. The Cotswold edge continues to twist and turn, and following a further fine edge-top walk, the Way comes out on to Crickley Hill, now considered a most important archaeological site and designated a country park. Settlements dating from 2500, 600, and 500BC have been excavated in recent summers and are interpreted on site.

In the next 'bay' between the promontories of Crickley Hill and Birdlip Peak is Barrow Wake, probably Gloucestershire's most visited viewpoint: beyond Gloucester, with its cathedral tower usually prominent, is May Hill, a dome-shaped hill with a clump of trees on top planted for Queen Victoria's Golden Jubilee. With reasonably good visibility, you can see the Sugar Loaf, Black Mountains and Brecon Beacons.

After crossing the Roman Ermine Street at Birdlip, the next 3 miles traverse the base of a steep slope which is covered in beech woods, a feature of valley sides in this part of the Cotswolds. At Cooper's Hill you look almost vertically up the slope down which, on Whit Mondays, hurtle brave souls who indulge in the ancient custom of chasing

Looking down to Painswick on the Cotswold Way (*British Tourist Authority*)

cheeses. Nearby, in an idyllic setting, is the modern Prinknash Abbey with its pottery and tearoom. Painswick Beacon is another of the delightful commons along the Cotswold edge over which we can roam, though as at Cleeve and Stinchcombe beware of golf balls whizzing through the air. No less than 15 miles of the Cotswold Way are over common land or over open space belonging to the National Trust or local authorities. In this case the views are not only across the Vale but also into the beautiful Painswick valley with its extensive beechwoods. Painswick itself is on the side of the valley and away from the Cotswold edge, but the Cotswold Way had to go through it as this is on many counts the most attractive village of all. The churchyard with its famous yew trees is particularly noteworthy. Opening up and waymarking the footpath route from Painswick back to the edge at, appropriately, the village of Edge, has presented many problems, not all yet resolved. Suffice to say that you should follow the guidebook at Washbrook Farm unless otherwise directed.

Another National Trust site, at Haresfield Beacon, gives one of the best viewpoints on the Way, this time bringing in the view to the south, with the Severn Bridge and estuary. The oldest and perhaps the most attractive of the many topographs along the Way is situated on the Shortwood promontory.

The deepest cut into the Cotswold escarpment by a side valley occurs in the Stroud district. Stroud itself is 3 miles from the edge and has valleys radiating from it like the tentacles of an octopus. The cloth mills now mostly make other products and are supplemented by other industries. The overspill from the narrow valleys filled much of the gap between Stroud and the Vale, but the Cotswold Way cuts through the less developed parts, crossing the derelict Stroudwater canal and passing a large woollen mill.

Once across the valley, tracks are followed along the lower slopes of beechwoods as far as Coaley Peak picnic site. Here a long barrow, with its burial-chamber stones open to the skies, contrasts with the tumulus previously seen at Belas Knap and with Hetty Pegler's Tump a mile further on, for which you have to collect a key to view the inside chambers. Between these archaeological features, the Gloucestershire Trust for Nature Conservation and the National Trust jointly protect the fauna and flora of the steep slopes of Frocester Hill.

The Cotswold Way near Dursley is very much a switchback, since instead of following the high edge, it follows a series of outliers, notably Cam Long Down (also appropriately know as Tableland) and Cam Peak, an intriguing conical-shaped hill. These hills, recently acquired by Stroud District Council, have panoramic views over the Vale and the secluded Uley valley, fringed with beechwoods. A steep climb from Dursley up to Stinchcombe golf course brings you to a remarkable plateau with views marred only by the M5 motorway and the continual drone therefrom.

Dropping through fields to North Nibley you climb again, to the monument to Tyndale, translator of the Bible. It is a rewarding climb up the spiral staircase to the viewing platform and a notice at the foot of the path tells you how to obtain the key in North Nibley. Unfortunately the key has to be returned there, so Cotswold Way walkers may prefer to make do with the view from ground level. Not to be missed is the old Cotswold wool town of Wotton-under-Edge with many interesting buildings and inns, particularly the fourteenth-century Old Ram Inn, now an unlicensed bed and breakfast house.

At Little Sodbury, a fine hill fort is traversed, this being only one of nine or so that are passed on the Cotswold Way, all in strategic places with commanding views. The escarpment is less pronounced in these southern parts of the Cotswolds; the height is generally 600 to 700ft, with less dramatic slopes than further north. Several of the villages are on a shelf part way down the slope. Thus North Nibley, Wotton and Old Sodbury are well above the plain below them. The Cotswold Way mainly follows field paths and there are few commons, or woodland walks. There are however fine country houses to visit, such as Dodington Park and Dyrham (National Trust), and the Way passes for a mile through the parkland at Dodington.

An incursion 'inland' is made to visit Cold Ashton, the last Cotswold stone village on the Way, then back to the edge after passing the monument to Sir Basil Grenville, slain in battle at nearby Lansdown. A sudden turn to the east puts the walker on the home straight for a descent into Bath via Sion Hill and the Royal Crescent, before reaching journey's end at the Roman baths and Bath Abbey.

Travelling to the Cotswold Way

Train services connect London to Bath, Stroud, Cheltenham, Moreton-in-Marsh, and Evesham. Stratford-upon-Avon can be reached from Birmingham, and the Birmingham to Bristol line runs parallel to the Cotswold Way. Chipping Campden is accessible by local bus from Stratford except on Sundays, but not from Moreton-in-Marsh or Evesham. Express coach services connect to Bath, Cheltenham and Broadway, and the latter passing two miles from Chipping Campden.

The Cotswold Way is well served by local bus services, either for reaching accommodation or for returning to a car parked at the start of a day's walk. This latter procedure is only difficult south of Wotton-under-Edge and north of Broadway. Most services are provided by Bristol Omnibus, but Castleways of Winchcombe operate between Cheltenham and Broadway, and Midland Red from Broadway and Chipping Campden.

Staying along the Way

Ramblers who prefer to stay the night where they finish their day's walk will find the Cotswold Way well provided with bed and breakfast establishments and country inns—the handbook lists eighty-five addresses. However, these are scarce near Stanway and Hawkesbury Upton. The Way is not at all well provided with youth hostels, and only Cleeve Hill is on the route, while Bath hostel is at one end. However, hostels at Slimbridge, Duntisbourne Abbots and Stow-on-the-Wold are only a few miles off the route and accessible by bus or road. Devoted hostellers will find that they can economise by using buses or thumbing a lift perhaps.

Camping is not easy on the Cotswold Way except on an informal basis. The few licensed sites are listed in the handbook and could be used by the motorised camping party, but the backpacker must seek permission to camp. Most farmers will allow a genuine backpacker to pitch a tent, draw water and maybe use toilet facilities, but remember, one case of abuse of these privileges is enough to make a farmer refuse in future.

Planning the daily walk

It is difficult to advise whether to walk south or north, as there are points in favour either way. The 97 mile route involves about 13,300ft of ascent going northwards, and 12,900ft going south. As the southern end is slightly less spectacular, and as the highest point, Cleeve Cloud, is nearer the north end, there is a sense of working up to a climax when going northwards. The theory about having the sun and prevailing wind behind you also favours a northward trek. On the other hand, if a Sunday return home by public transport is a consideration, then Bath is better served than Chipping Campden. The handbook gives a range of several walking schedules; here are three suggestions:

7 days plus 2 half days
To make the most of a week's holiday and both weekends, say Saturday midday to Sunday midday of the following week. The figures give mileages between points. Chipping Campden $5\frac{1}{2}$ Broadway $11\frac{3}{4}$

Winchcombe 10¾ A40, Dowdeswell Reservoir 13 Cooper's Hill 13¼ Kings Stanley 13¼ Wotton-under-Edge 12 Old Sodbury 10½ Grenville Monument 7 Bath.

8 days, making maximum use of youth hostels
The hostels used are in brackets. (Bath) Bath 9¾ Cold Ashton (Bath) 12¼ Hawkesbury Upton (bed and breakfast at Wotton-under-Edge) 10¼ North Nibley (Slimbridge) 11¾ Ryeford (Slimbridge) 14¾ Birdlip (Duntisbourne Abbots) 15¼ Cleeve Hill (Cleeve Hill) 11¾ Stanway (Stow-on-the-Wold or Cleeve Hill) 11¼ Chipping Campden (Stratford -upon-Avon).

8½ days using a car
With a folding bicycle used to return to the car at the end of each day. This schedule tries to ensure that the cycle ride is partly downhill or at least that there are no hills to cycle up. To this end, some sections are walked in the opposite direction to the general direction of travel, but all the ground is covered: (Day 1) Walk from Bath 7 miles to Grenville Monument (2) Old Sodbury 10½ to Grenville Monument (3) Old Sodbury 10½ to Newark Park (4) Kings Stanley 14¾ to Newark Park (5) Kings Stanley 10¾ to Painswick Beacon (6) Foot of Leckhampton Hill 12 to Painswick Beacon (7) Foot of Leckhampton Hill 10 to Cleeve Hill hostel (8) Stanway 11¾ to Cleeve Hill (9) Stanway 11¼ to Chipping Campden.

The Cotswold Way

Progressive Mileage	Miles Between	Places on route	Bus services	Cafes	Accommodation	Inns providing snacks etc	Shops
-	-	Chipping Campden	•	•	•	•	•
5½	5½	Broadway	•	•	•	•	•
11¼	5¾	Stanway	•	•	•		
13	1¾	Stumps Cross					
15	2	Hailes Abbey	1M				
17¼	2¼	Winchcombe	•	•	•	•	•
23	5¾	Cleeve Hill	•	•	•	•	
28	5	Dowdeswell Reservoir	•		•	•	
30½	2½	Seven Springs	•				
31½	1	Charlton Common	1M		1M	1M	1M
32½	1	Leckhampton Hill	•				1M
34	2½	Ullenwood Crossroads	•				
36½	2½	Crickley Hill	•			½M	
38¼	1¾	Birdlip	•		•	•	•
41	2¾	Coopers Hill	½M		1M		1M
42½	1½	Prinknash Corner	•				
43½	1	Painswick Beacon					
45	1½	Painswick	•	•	•	•	•
46½	1½	Edgemoor Inn	•			•	
49	2½	Haresfield Beacon					
53	4	Ryeford	•	¾M	¾M	¾M	¾M
54¼	1¼	Kings Stanley (Middleyard)			½M		½M
56½	2¼	Coaley Peak picnic site	•				
58	1½	Crawley Hill top	•		1M	1M	1M
60½	2½	Dursley	•		•	•	•
64¾	4¼	North Nibley	•		•		•
67½	2¾	Wotton-under-Edge	•		•	•	•
71¼	3¾	Alderley	•				
75	3¾	Hawkesbury Upton	•			•	•
77½	2½	Horton	•				
79½	2	Old Sodbury	•		•	•	•
82½	3	Tormarton M4 Interchange	•		•	½M	½M
85	2½	Dyrham Park (NT)		•			
86½	1½	Pennsylvania	•			•	
87¼	¾	Cold Ashton Turn	•				
90	2¾	Grenville Monument	1M				
91¼	1¼	Lansdown golfcourse	½M			½M	
94½	3¼	Weston	•				•
97	2½	Bath - Roman Baths	•	•	•	•	•

There are youth hostels at Bath and Cleeve Hill on the route, and at Slimbridge, Duntisbourne Abbots and Stow-on-the-Wold just a few miles off

Only Bath is actually served by rail but other stations, Evesham, Moreton in Marsh, Stratford, Cheltenham, Stroud and Stonehouse are within bus distance

The Ebor Way

Ken Piggin

The 70 mile Ebor Way links two other long-distance paths, joining the end (or the beginning, whichever way you look at it) of the Countryside Commission's Cleveland Way at Helmsley in north Yorkshire, with the Dales Way at Ilkley. In so doing, it also provides a link between the North York Moors and the Dales National Parks and the fine network of paths within these two areas.

The idea of this new route originated in July 1972 while the author was walking the Dales Way. Ramblers in Leeds and Harrogate were already forging ahead with their own link routes to join this splendid walk, so why not one from the ancient city of York itself? Over the year that followed a suitable route was decided on, but by that time, the idea of a further path to meet up with the Cleveland Way at Helmsley had been suggested.

After walking many alternative paths and discarding some to provide more interest and variety throughout the walk, a final route was established in August 1973. In trying out these alternatives we made many notes, visited interesting places, and took every opportunity of a friendly chat with farmers along the route. The majority were quite receptive to the idea when it was explained to them. In this way, over a period of three years, an idea for a link from York to Ilkley intended for a local rambling club in York, the Ebor Acorns, grew more by accident than design into a long-distance walk which could possibly be made available to all walkers.

Like many other such walks, we had planned it to use existing rights of way, but it did transpire later that we had trespassed for approximately 100yd! Two lessons were learnt, both of which have been confirmed by others who have completed the walk, and are worthy of note by intending walkers. Firstly, you should resist the temptation to cover too much ground in one day, even when the going might look to be easy. Even hardy walkers who have tackled marathons like the Lyke Wake Walk have found the 26 miles from Helmsley to York a shattering experience when attempted in one day. So take it easier! Secondly, you should go well prepared when walking through growing crops, particularly in late August and September when the corn is high. After a shower of rain you can get soaked faster than, say, walking through wet bracken on the moors, so consider gaiters and waterproofs essential if you want to keep dry.

Between 1976 and March 1978, when the guide was published, some waymarking was done, particularly at the northern end where route-finding had proved a little difficult in those early days. One of the ramblers who tackled the walk that year, Tony Galvin from Beverley, then produced the Ebor Way signs in oak which are now to be seen along the path. As soon as the guide was out, we began to hear from many others who had completed the walk; from ladies, a boy of eleven who walked it with his father, from novices trying their first long-distance expedition, and from experienced long-distance walk enthusiasts. Coming from as far afield as London, Birmingham, Hull and Glasgow, they all expressed their appreciation at discovering this wonderful countryside and its friendly inhabitants. Of course, someone must always go for a record, and we have even heard from a walker who has covered the Way in 20 hours, including $18\frac{1}{2}$ hours of walking. Not to be recommended if you want to pause to admire the beauty of the scenery!

Many have asked about the origins of the name. Eboracum, shortened to Ebor, was the Roman name for York, adopted by the rambling club and then applied also to the walking route they pioneered. The Ebor Way Pioneers hold an annual reunion every October at the Bay Horse in Terrington, where most of the locals regard us as old friends. It is significant that our walk has brought no complaints at all from farmers or landowners. I was also very pleased to note while walking the Way in the autumn of 1978, that many improvements had been made, new bridges and stiles provided, and above all, not one scrap of litter could I find along the path. Remarkable achievements, of which both countryfolk and walkers can be justly proud.

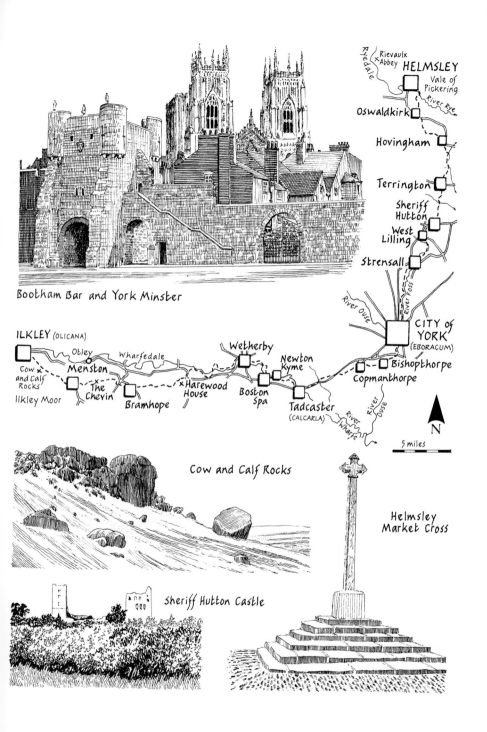

Bootham Bar and York Minster

Cow and Calf Rocks

Helmsley Market Cross

Sheriff Hutton Castle

Between Helmsley and Ilkley the Way passes through delightful countryside and, although the highest point is only 1000ft above sea level and that almost at the end of the walk, the walker will find that the top of every hill provides splendid views around. Through extensive areas of woodland and rolling country, over arable land, along riverside paths and over tiny streams, the whole varied wildlife of the countryside is around you. Almost every town and village on the Way is worth an hour or two of exploration, with many a fine old church, ruins of castles, and friendly inns where the landlord will provide a wealth of local information.

Helmsley to York

Helmsley, the starting point of the walk, is one of north Yorkshire's most attractive small towns, with the castle ruins standing guard over stone houses, shops and inns surrounding the market place. The castle stands to the west of the town, an impressive reminder of the Civil War for it was here in 1644 that the Royalists were besieged by the Parliamentarians. After a siege lasting several months, they surrendered and the castle was dismantled by order of parliament. The town, on the edge of the North York Moors National Park, is a popular base for exploring the surrounding moors and valleys on foot.

After a 2 mile walk along the tiny river Rye, the path turns southward through the well-wooded area of rolling countryside known as the Howardian Hills. These small hills will make you puff a little, but will also provide the excuse for a breather and a look round at the splendid countryside. A mixture of broad-leaved and coniferous trees provide a habitat for many birds, while the open countryside between is the home of the skylark, pheasant and partridge. Grey squirrels abound in the woods between Hovingham and Terrington, where you will also see several species of fungi including the inedible pink-coloured variety called 'sickener'.

Some 8 miles from Helmsley and almost in the middle of this stretch of country is Hovingham, one of the prettiest villages on the walk with its stone-built cottages standing alongside a stream spanned by tiny bridges. The magnificent hall built in 1760 is the seat of the Worsley

Members of the Long Distance Walkers Association follow the Ebor Way near
Terrington (*Ken Piggin*)

family, and was the scene of a very important discovery in 1745 when,
during excavations, a Roman bath with a roof of polished perforated
tiles and tesselated pavement was found, along with fragments of
Roman pottery and coins. Just before Hovingham village, the walk
passes Hovingham Spa, now derelict except for the well-kept house,
but a scene of great activity during the nineteenth century when the
three springs gave forth water reputed to cure rheumatism.

Three miles of good walking with some grand views northward to
the moors and westward over the Vale of York, and you arrive at the
village of Terrington. Another delightful unspoilt village, it has a very
interesting old church and the Bay Horse, venue for the annual reunion of the Pioneers and which also provides bed and breakfast and
meals. Shortly after leaving the village, the Way leaves the Howardian
Hills and passes through an area which in bygone days was part of the
forest of Galtres. This was no forest in today's terms, but rather the
type of terrain found at Strensall, unreclaimed land with coarse grasses
and considerable areas of woodland. The principal tree was the giant
oak and even now the broad-leaf trees flourish here. Oak, ash, sycamore

and chestnuts are prevalent and, wherever the land is marshy, the willow.

Although the area is flat, the walk is certainly not dull and you will find a great deal of interest between here and York. The next village is Sheriff Hutton, with its ruined castle standing against the skyline. The ancient village church dedicated to St Helen and the Holy Cross has some good brasses, and box pews dating from the 1830s. In the chapel of St Nicholas is a memorial to Edward, Prince of Wales, the son of King Richard III who died at Middleham when eleven years old. The castle was built in the late fourteenth century by Lord John Neville and owned in 1484 by Queen Anne, daughter of the Earl of Warwick. Although the castle stands in private grounds in the middle of a farmyard, the present owner does not object to visitors inspecting the ruins—providing of course that permission is obtained and the place treated with respect.

Approaching the next village on the Way, Strensall, the walk passes through a nature reserve, an area of unreclaimed heathland which is noted for its ground-loving insects, reptiles and ground nesting birds. Grasshoppers and dragonflies are plentiful, and there is a rich variety of beetles, moths and butterflies. In Strensall there are shops and a couple of pubs. Then for most of the remainder of the journey into York, we follow the river Foss, skirting the villages of Haxby, Huntington and New Earswick in the process. Just beyond New Earswick is a pleasant little cottage called Lock House, standing alongside the remains of one of the locks used when the Foss was navigable beyond Strensall. From this point we can see York Minster towering above the city ahead. A further $1\frac{1}{2}$ miles, most of it along the riverside path, brings us to Monk Bar, one of the four great bars which guarded the entrances to the city.

The walk continues along the bar walls, and anyone wishing to do so could continue thus across the city and only meet one road on the way. Only the walker in a desperate hurry is likely to do this however, for York is a wonderful place with much to see. The city has a history that can be traced back to its foundation in AD 71, a fortress which the Romans called Eboracum and which became one of their most important cities. Many of the Roman governors of Britain lived here, and Constantine the Great was born and proclaimed ruler of the western provinces of the Roman empire within these walls. A very small part of the fourth-century fortress wall can be seen in St Leonards, and the multangular tower which stood at the south-west corner of the fortress is now in the museum gardens. In the Yorkshire Museum, many Roman relics from York and the surrounding district are on view. With so many other places of interest in the city—the Minster, Shambles, Castle Museum and National Railway Museum to mention a few—no doubt many walkers along the Ebor Way will be planning their schedule to allow some time for exploring York.

York to Ilkley

Between York and Tadcaster, the walking is flat but certainly not uninteresting. A couple of miles along the river Ouse brings you to Bishopthorpe and the palatial home of the Archbishop of York, with its fine gatehouse adorned with battlements, pinnacles and gargoyles. The church was replaced in 1799, and the remains of the old church are to be found in a beautiful corner beside the river, the west front standing in all its former glory and the site of the altar marked by a cross. The area abounds with wild life and it is not uncommon to see squirrels running along the fence beside the path. The woods here are alive with birds, including the grasshopper and willow warbler, the spotted flycatcher, great spotted woodpecker and kingfisher, as well as many of the tit and finch families. Stoats and weasels are plentiful and there have been sightings of fallow deer, thought to have wandered along the river from Escrick Park.

On through Copmanthorpe where centuries ago the Knights Templars held much of the land, the Way follows the line of the Roman road known as the Old Street. This takes us almost all the way to Tadcaster, another spot with a long history dating back to the Brigantes. As a military outpost for the Romans stationed at York, it was called Calcaria and was reached by fording the river at a point just before the weir. The riverside path which Ebor Way walkers use was a trench that served as a defence during the Civil War. The Ark Museum, a well-preserved fifteenth-century house, has a collection of items of local interest, particularly those connected with the brewing trade for which the town is famous.

At Tadcaster, the Way joins the river Wharfe and from here to Ilkley the river is very rarely out of view as we follow riverside walks with their luxuriant foliage, or the side of hills with extensive views over the rolling countryside of lower Wharfedale. After a very pleasant stretch along the river, the walk passes through a tiny village, Newton Kyme, which probably contains more of interest per acre than any other place on the route. Within half a mile you will pass a well cared-for church, part Norman, with many features including a fascinating squint opening; then the remains of a castle in the grounds of the impressive hall where Admiral Robert Fairfax once lived, and a well-restored tithe barn down the road.

The riverside walk is regained by following a route which the Romans trod many centuries ago. This rough track is Rudgate, part of the Roman road which linked Doncaster (Danum) with Aldborough (Isurium). It crossed the Wharfe at St Helen's Ford, named after the mother of Constantine the Great.

The beauty of the riverside scene at Boston Spa, the next place on the Way, is not surpassed anywhere along the lower Wharfe; in fact only those walkers who turn off to avail themselves of the facilities there, will realise that a very large and busy village is just a few yards from the walk. Over the narrow bridge is the tiny village of Thorp Arch, much older than its neighbour as it is mentioned in Domesday book as Torp. The church, quite a distance from the village, is well worth a visit. The woodwork has been renewed by Mr Thompson of Kilburn whose famous mouse emblem can be seen on the pews and various other parts of the church.

The walk from Thorp Arch to Wetherby is a pleasant one in dry weather, but the path passes through a farmyard and in very wet weather walkers will find themselves plodding through a mixture of mud and other farmyard material which can leave them with a lingering country smell! Wetherby is a town with quite a history, a summary of which is thoughtfully provided on a plaque attached to the town hall. Once held by the Knights Templars, it was a very busy place in the old coaching days, being a midway stop between London and Edinburgh.

Soon after leaving Wetherby you will see a change in the countryside as the flat lands of the Vale of York give way to the rolling country and

Back-packing (*British Tourist Authority*)

woodland typical of lower Wharfedale. Woodhall Ecumenical Centre is 3 miles beyond Wetherby in 190 acres of this lovely countryside overlooking the Wharfe, with our walk passing through the grounds. Walkers are welcome here—a letter was received expressing the hope that the Way would be a success—but please remember that this is a religious establishment and you should pass through quietly, particularly by the convent.

A walk along a fine stretch of the Wharfe brings you to Harewood. Here the remains of Sir William Aldburgh's medieval castle, built soon after the Conquest and reconstructed in the reign of Edward III, stand high on the hill overlooking the river. Harewood House, seat of the Earl of Harewood, is open to the public, as also are 150 acres of pleasure gardens, a lake and wonderful bird gardens which contain some 200 species of bird. The park however covers some 1,800 acres in total, and it is through this area that the Ebor Way passes. First place of interest is the church, famous for its collection of alabaster tombs on which rest the effigies of former members of the Harewood family. Entering the park, you will suddenly become aware of the spectacular scenery you will be enjoying for the rest of the journey. Ahead and slightly to the right, Almscliff Crag rises majestically over the village of Weeton and ahead, mere outlines against the sky as yet, are the Chevin and Rombalds Moor, the end of the Way. In the rich parkland cows and sheep graze in contentment, and the old oaks provide cover for pheasants and squirrels.

A pleasant walk on a high-level track gives a splendid view of the village of Arthington and the viaduct carrying the Leeds to Harrogate railway. It brings us to the village of Bramhope, where the tiny Puritan chapel is worth a visit. Built between 1646 and 1649, it is one of only two chapels of its kind in the country.

Through the grounds of the National Childrens' Home there are open views and you can see the White Horse of Kilburn on a clear day. Now the walk continues through an afforested area, the Danesfield estate, where the wide tracks provide splendid walking and views over the Washburn valley, good walking country and well worth a visit. Ahead lies 2 miles of even better views, and some say that Otley Chevin has some of the finest views in England. The panorama across the Vale

Almscliffe Crag from Otley Chevin

of York to the east competes with that to the Craven moors to the west, and down below the velvet green patchwork quilt which surrounds the town of Otley.

The walk leads on through Menston to Burley Woodhead and to the climax of the whole expedition, the stiff climb up Barks Crag. Up and down, over streams and past waterfalls, the path arrives at the Cow and Calf where you can stand and survey most of the landmarks along the Ebor Way. Temptingly too, there is a good view of upper Wharfedale, where the Dales Way continues on to Bowness-on-Windermere. Through Ilkley the Ebor Way finally ends at the old pack-horse bridge over the Wharfe. Beside it stands the sign pointing the way along the Dales Way, an open invitation to continue on the longer walk to the shores of Lake Windermere.

How should you set out to walk the Ebor Way? For quite long distances the Way uses good tracks which will present few problems, but walkers should go prepared, for there are extensive areas of arable land between Helmsley and Tadcaster which can prove difficult and uncomfortable in wet weather. Even beyond Tadcaster the riverside paths can be muddy at times, so always wear good strong boots and if you can, invest in a pair of gaiters. They will provide that added protection needed when walking through long grass or standing crops. Most of the paths are signposted now as they leave the public road, but only part of the northern section is waymarked at present, by standard pattern small arrows supplemented occasionally by oak signs. One day soon perhaps, West Riding will waymark the remainder of the route in similar fashion.

We know that it is possible to complete the whole route within 24 hours, but really this is a walk to take your time over, spending a while here and there to explore. If the walk is being tackled as a continuous exercise, a week would be preferable. But if there is more time available, take a fortnight over it, enjoy a little walking off the main route perhaps, and spend more time at Helmsley, York or Ilkley.

A number of people who have completed the Ebor Way have asked for information on other walks in this attractive area. There are several guides I can recommend for those who intend to adventure a little further afield, or do some circular walks based on the Way. One book, *Walks North of York*, for example, describes fifteen walks from 3 to $11\frac{1}{2}$ miles in the Howardian Hills, three of them using a part of the Way. Another, *Walks in the Vale of York*, describes fourteen short walks, two of them partly along the Way and others starting from Copmanthorpe and Tadcaster. *Wetherby and Tadcaster Footpath Walks* is a first-class guide to twenty walks, most of them circular, in the area between Copmanthorpe and Harewood. Three of them are along parts of the Ebor Way. The *Otley and District Footpath Map and Guide* is an excellent 1:25 000 scale map showing field boundaries, gates and stiles, etc., and of course the Ebor Way, from Bramhope to Ilkley, with brief descriptions of a number of easy walks.

After you have walked the Ebor Way, remember that this author would welcome a report from you, as these provide useful information on any problems encountered. To improve the service to future walkers, details of accommodation (even the places you didn't like) and spots along the route where camping is allowed, are all very useful. I can supply Ebor Way badges and completion cards, the profits from which are donated to Hilton Grange School for handicapped children, a branch of the National Childrens' Homes. Your walk will have taken you through the grounds of the school, and you may already have met the children enjoying the countryside along their part of the Ebor Way.

The Ebor Way

Progressive Mileage	Miles Between	Places on route	Bus service to	Rail Service	Cafes	Accommodation	Inns providing snacks etc	Shops	Camping
-	-	Helmsley	Thirsk, Ripon, Scarborough		●	●	●	●	
4	4	Oswaldkirk	Helmsley, Hovingham				●	●	
8	4	Hovingham	Helmsley, Malton				●	●	Allowed at Airyholme Farm
11½	3½	Terrington	Malton		●	●	●		
15	3½	Sheriff Hutton	York		●	●	●		
20	5	Strensall	York local services			●	●		
23	3	Haxby	As above			●	●	●	
27	4	York	As above	●	●	●	●	●	
31	4	Bishopthorpe	As above			●	●	●	Riverside site
33	2	Copmanthorpe	As above				●	●	
38	5	Tadcaster	York, Leeds, Wetherby		●	●	●	●	
42	4	Boston Spa	Tadcaster, Wetherby			●	●	●	
45	3	Wetherby	Tadcaster, Leeds, Harrogate		●	●	●	●	Racecourse camp site
55	10	Harewood	Leeds, Harrogate					●	
59	4	Bramhope	Leeds, Bradford, Otley				●	●	
64	5	Menston	Leeds, Otley	●			●	●	Camp site at end of Otley Chevin
70	6	Ilkley	Otley, Leeds, Bradford, Harrogate	●	●	●	●	●	

There are youth hostels at Helmsley, Malton and York

Early closing: Helmsley, York, Tadcaster, Wetherby, Otley and Ilkley all close on Wednesday afternoon

The Thames Walk

David Sharp

The broad Thames as it flows beneath the London bridges is beyond question one of the world's great rivers. Already its waters have glimpsed the spires of Oxford and Eton college, seen the great battlements of Windsor Castle against the skyline, and the chimneys and pinnacles of Hampton Court. Not to mention the modest Cotswold stone of Kelmscott Manor where William Morris thought out his reformist ideals. But stand on Putney Bridge and as you gaze upstream you are, probably without knowing it, contemplating the start of a journey that could take you by towpath and remote footpath to the source of Old Father Thames in the foothills of the Cotswolds. A walk that attracts a special few every year, for the love of strolling by rivers and exploring to the very meadow where, just occasionally when the water table allows, the Thames spring rises. A fascinating but alas rather frustrating walk, for historical reasons that require explanation.

By Putney Bridge and virtually at your feet, the old Thames towpath begins its journey to Lechlade. At first, past the boathouses that mark the start of the Universities boat-race course, the towpath does not stand out, but you can see it distantly as a pleasant gravel path with open playing fields to one side, the river to the other. Almost a country walk in the heart of London! Indeed, as it swings around the first great curve towards Barnes, the walk becomes so rural and profuse with greenery that even the Thames vanishes from view at times. This is one considerable virtue of our towpath—surely there is no other way of walking out of London so pleasantly. Today the towpath is used no more for towing. Instead it has the status of a public footpath for almost all of its 130 mile length. It would be ideal for our purposes, were it not for the habit the towpath has of changing banks from time to time.

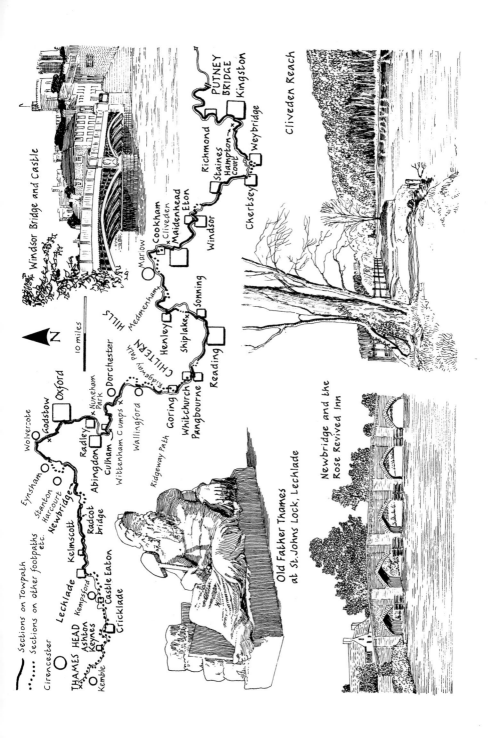

Sections on Towpath

Sections on other footpaths etc.

Cirencester

THAMES HEAD

Kemble

Ashton Keynes

Cricklade

Castle Eaton

Kempsford

Lechlade

Kelmscott

Radcot bridge

Newbridge

Stanton Harcourt

Eynsham

Wolvercote

Godstow

Oxford

Radley

Abingdon

Culham

× Nuneham Park

Dorchester

Wittenham Cumps ×

Wallingford

Ridgeway Path

Goring

Whitchurch

Pangbourne

Reading

Sonning

Shiplake ×

Henley

CHILTERN HILLS

Medmenham

Marlow

Cookham

Cliveden

Maidenhead

Eton

Windsor

Chertsey

Weybridge

Staines

Hampton Court

Richmond

PUTNEY BRIDGE

Kingston

N

10 miles

Windsor Bridge and Castle

Cliveden Reach

Old Father Thames at St. Johns Lock, Lechlade

Newbridge and the Rose Revived Inn

The reason is that, for much of the 1,000 year period during which barges struggled to carry their cargoes up river to Oxford or even to Lechlade, the Thames lacked any effective authority. It was not until the late eighteenth century that Conservators were appointed to carry out long-needed improvements, including the establishment of a continuous towpath. Created at this late date, and along the banks of a natural river, it met a host of problems. Shallows, islands and marshy ground that would have fouled the tow, unhelpful riparian landowners who refused to accept the towpath, or who charged exorbitantly for towing rights, and of course riverside development—all were reasons for the towpath changing to the more convenient bank. All too often this was done by ferry, and not one of these navigation ferries operate today. Their names, like Roebuck, Keen Edge, Chalmore Hole, My Lady, Beetle and Wedge, Bablock Hythe, are fast vanishing from the maps, even from memory, and nothing remains but a few traces of a landing stage or a lonely ferry cottage. So the walker following the towpath finds himself gazing across the river to where his walk continues on the other bank.

The concept of a continuous walk along the Thames is not new, indeed it was much debated in the 1950s. The old Thames Conservancy realised that they had a towpath no longer needed in its original role, but with exciting possibilities for public recreation. The newly established National Parks Commission had the Thames on its list for consideration as one of the long-distance routes it had powers to set up, and naturally the two bodies got together. To no avail though, as it seemed the task of restoring a neglected towpath and maintaining ferries or their substitutes, was too expensive for the day. So the idea was put aside, for occasional dusting down and reconsideration—and meanwhile, as the last of the Thames ferries closed, the walk actually grew more difficult and discontinuous than ever.

Yet interest never died, and in 1973 the River Thames Society, an influential amenity body, held a conference in Windsor to look at the subject anew. From this conference came the realisation that officialdom really would do nothing, and indeed so many authorities were involved along the Thames that it was perhaps unreasonable to expect any one to shoulder the problems of a 156 mile long path. So the Ramblers'

Association stepped in and began their own survey, a three-year job involving five local Ramblers' groups along the river, resulting in the publication of an impressive planning study in 1977. We called it simply, the Thames Walk.

Soon after publication we heard from ramblers who had tackled the problems with surprising enterprise. One had swum across the ferry stages, towing his rambling gear behind him in a plastic bag. Another had inflated a rubber dinghy to paddle his family across, an unusual mixture of boating and rambling that everyone claimed to have enjoyed. But our survey had to find more prosaic solutions, and did so by tracing the best diversions it could find along other footpaths and roads near the river, to link one section of towpath to a point where the errant towpath could be taken up again. The very first problem point upstream can well illustrate this approach. Having followed the towpath without a hitch as far as the pleasant loops of the old Thames channel by Shepperton, you will find yourself opposite Shepperton Lock where, because of the complex entry of the river Wey on our bank, the towpath changes to the far bank. What happens next? Undeterred, we leave the river by an unexpected little discovery of an urban path, undoubtedly an old church path that the houses of Weybridge have never been allowed to consume. Turning from this, we cross a footbridge over a muddy branch of the Wey, then by an unprepossessing squeeze between factory walls to a sudden and total surprise—a little lock and lock cottage on much too small a scale for the Thames. And indeed this is the Wey Navigation. Cross the bridge above the lock, follow its towpath for an idyllic half mile, then leave it to find the line of a footpath over Chertsey Mead back to the Thames at Chertsey, where we can cross and regain our own towpath walk. Even the Mead has interest—the wide flood plain of the Thames, drained by the Bourne stream with a pronounced terrace above it.

So by diversions and contrivances like this, the Thames Walk manages to take you to Lechlade and on to the source. Some of the diversions are very fine—for example, the walk over Winter Hill gives one of the best of all views over the Thames valley to Bourne End and the Chilterns. Others, alas, have to take you along busy roads for a while. Today's Thames Walk is far from perfect and the survey made many proposals for improvement. New lengths of public path, very short lengths in several cases, would provide needed links, and there are two points where it would be desirable to be able to cross the river by lock and weir, in substitute for the nearby ferry that no longer runs. Year by year, we should begin to see these improvements come to pass.

Our Thames Walk seems to divide naturally into three sections, with a clear change of character as the river passes from one to another.

The popular Thames

From Putney to Oxford, the river is a well-used waterway and through the summer months our walk will be accompanied most of the while by the thrum of outboard motors as the cruiser traffic passes. Quiet stretches there are, but punctuated by busy centres like Cookham, Marlow or Henley, where the river comes alive with Englishmen messing around in boats, and the Thames seems to inspire everyone to find ways of enjoying its benign presence. Here are the famous spots, the Thames at Sonning, the Thames at Whitchurch, and other colour calendar views, and the visitor will certainly want to turn from the towpath to explore Windsor and Oxford at the least.

An important feature of this length of Thames is the excellent public transport back to London from point after point. As far as Windsor there are services too numerous to mention; then the Great Western line takes over, the broad gauge route that Brunel drove to the West Country, following the Thames Valley with stations at Maidenhead, Reading, Pangbourne, Goring, Cholsey and Didcot. Branch lines still serve Marlow and Henley, and even Oxford is only an hour from London. So, with a check of bus and train times, it is easy enough to divide the Thames Walk into lengths of your own choosing, to walk a section and return to London.

A first day's walk will take you perhaps to Kingston, past the Regency elegance of Richmond and the fine red-brick seventeenth-century river frontage of Ham House. Already you will have found a surprisingly green rural walk past Kew Gardens and by Ham Fields, and maybe turned along a tempting footpath to find the first of many Thames 'gems', little Petersham church with its lantern tower and

The Thames Walk passes Bray Lock on the way to Maidenhead (*David Sharp*)

lovely interior of box pews and galleries. Beyond Kingston, the towpath takes for a while the more pretentious title of Barge Walk, to swing grandly round Hampton Court Park to the palace itself. Plebeian towpath walkers view the Wren river frontage through the superb wrought-iron garden screen by Tijou. Then on by riverside Sunbury and Walton to try out the charming diversion by the Wey Navigation, already described, to Staines. No great beauty abounds here, but soon the Thames flows through the meadows of Runnymede. Our old river has seen great events here, and somehow even the cars and picnic parties cannot quell the sense of significance conveyed by these willow lined pastures. Then to Albert Bridge, and our philosophising on Magna Carta, the monarchy, and the rights of the people come to an abrupt halt as we face the road tramp around by Datchet village to avoid the towpath closed through Windsor Home Park. Back on the river bank again by Romney Lock, Windsor Castle provides the backdrop across playing fields. Over Windsor Bridge the walk takes to the riverside meadow of Brocas, with the finest of views back to the great castle, rising over the rooftops. Now comes the wildest part of the walk yet, as the river skirts the vast open field of Dorney. As Maidenhead approaches, we meet the Great Western line in spectacular fashion as it crosses the river by Brunel's sounding arch. This graceful curve of bridge is actually the widest, flattest arch of brick in the world, spanning 128ft with a rise of only 24ft. A masterpiece, but later we will walk under an equally fine angled bridge by Brunel at Moulsford.

Beyond is Boulter's Lock, busiest and best known of all the Thames locks, where you can join the summer crowds watching the boats, and recall favourite passages from *Three Men in a Boat*. Cliveden reach is superb, the beechwoods rising steeply from the far bank, and glimpses of the house of Cliveden itself until we reach the old My Lady ferry landing and turn by footpath into Cookham village. Around the open curve of Cock Marsh, the Thames often speckled with the white sails of dinghies out from Bourne End, a little white house appears ahead which is Spade Oak ferry cottage. We leave the river and bypass Marlow entirely now, but the views from Winter Hill and the shady tracks down through Quarry Woods have their compensations. Temple, where we at last regain the Thames, brings us immediately to Hurley village, one of those riverside spots that only the most dedicated footslogger will pass by without exploring. Rustic wooden bridges carry the towpath over to the lock island and back. Little tree-hung footpaths lead to the village street, with the remains of Hurley Priory, a fourteenth-century barn and a dovecote to be found. Only a mile or so further on, and you are looking across the river to Medmenham Abbey, creeper-clad Gothic style of many dates, but so well blended as to be quite the most romantically picturesque house along the Thames. Again at Medmenham, the tiny landing stage reminds us of a ferry that can be hailed no more, but a convenient riverside path takes us on to Aston and thence to Henley. This is a superb reach of the Thames, with old weather-boarded Hambledon Mill across its weirs, and the Chiltern hills beyond.

Above Henley, missing ferries again take us on a diversion through the lanes of riverside Shiplake until we can regain the river at Shiplake Lock. Like a fickle lady, the Thames first turns its would-be faithful followers aside in this fashion, then repeatedly rewards us with one of its most glorious stretches. So it is with this Shiplake walk. The subtle composition of trees, islands and sloping meadow, lock and ever-present river, is an inspiration for the artist and photographer.

The towpath passing Remenham on the Henley reach. The distant white temple on its island marks the end of the regatta course (*David Sharp*)

Sonning is another riverside village to explore, large and well kept, with a whimsical bridge of eleven brick arches, every one a different size it seems. Then Reading, and with the approach of a major township you might well expect the Thames to vanish into miles of dull urbanisation. Not so—both Reading and Oxford treat the river most courteously, keeping their distance with discretion and bringing a mere mile or less of building to the river bank. No sooner have we walked under Caversham bridge than Reading is behind us, the towpath green and pleasant, and the Chilterns in view again across the river.

Opposite Purley is a quite unique length of towpath that we cannot, by any ingenuity, use. Two centuries ago, a Purley landowner forced the towpath over to the north bank for a quarter mile. The bargemen cursed this, and so do we as we divert round by the houses of Purley to get back to the river. But there still, on the Mapledurham bank, is that quarter mile of towpath, a public right of way with no access except by boat. At Pangbourne, knowing that the ferry ahead is missing, the Walk takes to Chiltern tracks through Hartslock Wood, determined to regain the river at Gatehampton so that we can follow the river

Aston Ferry near Henley

through the famous Goring Gap, with Chiltern chalk on one hand and the Berkshire Downs rising steeply on the other. Above Goring, the Thames Walk joins up for a while with another long-distance walk, the Ridgeway Path. Together they pass by Cleeve Mill and the two pretty Stoke villages, South and North, but while the Ridgeway walkers turn as they reach the ancient Grims Ditch, to trace it towards the Chilterns escarpment, we stay faithful to the Thames and follow it to Wallingford.

Alas, there are more diversions ahead: first, a tramp round to Preston Crowmarsh village, because of the missing ferry at Benson. By compensation the first thatch appears here, and soon a much more pleasant little footpath diversion takes us away from the Thames again to the quite delightful single street of Shillingford. The street leads straight and abruptly to the river—was this the 'ford' of the village name? Then the Thame enters the Thames, lazily, with many loops and wriggles, and we cross by footbridge to reach Little Wittenham. If a 'most beautiful' label had to be awarded amongst Thames landscapes, this spot would probably win. The bare Sinodun Hills rise above Little Wittenham woods, twin beech clumps crowning them. Below, the Thames curves beneath the footbridge to the village, with Days Lock and its weir completing the picture upstream. A spot to linger and absorb, then perhaps to take the steep path up the nearer hill. These summits that rise so abruptly from the valley give superb views.

Clifton Hampden around the next great curve of the Thames is a village of fine thatch, even running to two thatched picture-book pubs, and a red-brick bridge that replaced the ferry here in Victorian times. All along this reach, the vast grey forms of Didcot power station act as backdrop to the river. By Abingdon you have said goodbye to it, and suddenly you meet the most glorious of all the riverside townscapes. Abingdon presents us with lines of mellow seventeenth- and eighteenth-century almshouses (does any other town have so many?), all reflected in Thames water, with the spire of St Helens church as focal point to the scene. I can never turn that last bend which reveals the composition of Abingdon without a sense of uplift. We do not seem able to create an entity like this any more.

Pause and explore a while at Abingdon, for now comes a total break in the riverside walk. Again, a missing ferry is the culprit, and short of trespass we can only suggest taking the Oxford bus on to Radley where the towpath can be regained. At least from Radley on, the walk to Oxford is easy and enjoyable. Sandford is passed on the way, an isolated little industrial group of red-brick mill, lock and cottages. At Iffley, the public way across lock and weir could be taken to visit the superb Norman church, rich in zigzag Romanesque carving. Then, almost before you expect it, the Oxford colleges are in view over Christchurch Meadow, with one or two of the ornate college barges moored by the bank. If you are observant you will have spotted several more of these barges along the river near Oxford, some of them converted into houseboats. Pity that so few can be seen here by Christchurch Meadow, where they would make such a fine show.

The Thames Walk comes to Abingdon, with almshouses and the spire of St Helen's church across the Thames (*David Sharp*)

The remote Thames

Leaving urban Oxford, you will come to Osney Bridge. On it, a notice warns that clearance is only 7ft 7in, a dire restricting obstacle to owners of tall river craft. In its way too, an inspired gateway to the further Thames reaches upstream, so different to the busy, populated river we have known so far. For 20 miles now, up to Lechlade, no town or village stands on the river. All the communities are high and dry on the gravel heights well back from the Thames, looking out over the wide flood plain. Eynsham, Stanton Harcourt, Northmoor, Appleton, Longworth, Buckland, Aston, Bampton and Faringdon, all keep their distance, although perhaps we should think of them as townships and villages of the Thames. On the river itself, only the occasional lock-house or the inn, established to serve a river trade, keep us company. Except for the occasional bus out of Oxford to Swinford Bridge or Appleton to help us on our way, we are leaving public transport behind. Instead we will probably plan an overnight stop at Newbridge, or one of the many hostelries of Bampton, reached by footpaths over the polder land from Rushy Lock.

Very soon after crossing Osney Bridge and heading upstream, we enter a landscape that has not changed through many centuries. Over the Thames lies Port Meadow, a vast common field given to Oxford by William the Conqueror. Cows, geese and ponies can still be seen grazing here by the riverside, while on our own bank the tiny hamlet of Binsey has an equally ancient feel, standing by its own parcel of green. Then Godstow with its ruined nunnery and far from ruined Trout Inn, and soon the Evenlode is slipping quietly into the Thames opposite us. Each of the Cotswold streams with their enchanting, evocative names, will be coming down to the river from here on. At Northmoor, we might pause to see the first weir that still uses the primitive wooden paddles that are fast vanishing even from the upper Thames; they belong to a bygone age. Ahead now, a lonely bridge spans the river, Harts Weir footbridge. These early crossings tell us much about the importance of public ways. You will see no weir at this spot today, but through the centuries a right of way was established across it, linking communities across the valley. When the weir was finally taken up, the right of way had to be maintained by the building of a footbridge, and both here, and at Tenfoot and Old Man's footbridge further upstream, we have picturesque reminders of weirs that are no more.

Newbridge, in contradiction of its name, is thirteenth century and possibly the oldest bridge along the river. A most beautiful bridge too, with its rising arches of mellow stone, handsomely composed with an inn of matching stone at either end. Pause at least for a Morelands bitter at the Maybush where even the sign is a thing of beauty, then on to Duxford where an unused loop of the river leads to a genuine Thames ford, still fordable in dry weather. A delectable spot this, where willows frame the rippling waters and local lads play in the stream. From Rushy, where we follow the towpath over lock and weir, the walk is through lush riverside meadows, filled with buttercups in summer. For company you have the herds of sprightly little heifers who are quite delighted to find visitors in their Thames-side homelands, and gallop up to inspect you. They seem to regard rucksacks as a rare delicacy, but are otherwise harmless!

The towpath walk reaches St John's Lock, highest on the Thames, with Lechlade in the distance (*David Sharp*)

Kelmscott from the towpath is no more than a tree-framed glimpse of the lovely sixteenth-century stone manor house that was the home of William Morris for twenty-five years. But wander through the straggling village and find in the churchyard the stone slab, most moving in its simplicity, under which Morris lies buried. He would be happy to see how little has changed here. Now the spire of Lechlade church ahead beckons us on, and at St Johns Lock we meet Father Thames himself. The reclining statue by the lock house began life in the Crystal Palace grounds, then presided over the source at Thames Head for a while, and now for safety has come to live out his days at the highest lock on the river.

The unknown Thames

Just above Lechlade our towpath finally ends. Over the river can just be traced the overgrown entry and roundhouse that was once the Thames & Severn Canal, and that way went the towpath. From here on we must follow ordinary footpaths as best we can to the source, and as the river traffic also stops at Lechlade, it is only the rambler who can explore this uppermost Thames. The first few hundred yards bring us to a most marvellous find. The stone building we have seen across the riverside meadow reveals itself as Inglesham church, a tiny thirteenth-century building quite untouched and perfect. William Morris loved it and defended it from the restorers. Inside, the seventeenth-century box pews are warped at every angle.

From here on, we shall see only glimpses of the infant Thames, as old trackways and paths take us on to Castle Eaton. Every time we meet the river it seems a little diminished, at Hannington Bridge, then as it flows by Castle Eaton church, and finally at Water Eaton footbridge where we can take a fisherman's path on to Cricklade. As the Thames flows by the foot of Cricklade High Street, it is narrow enough to be bridged by a convenient telegraph pole. A path leads on beyond the little town to North Meadow Nature Reserve, where the infant Thames meets this jealously preserved meadow. Looking back, the massive Tudor tower of St Samsons, Cricklade, can be seen over the modest stream that is now the Thames, forming a succession of views that Constable would have loved to paint. Ashton Keynes is a rambling stone village reached by quiet lanes, through which the Thames flows by several routes. Along one village road, every farmstead has its own bridge over the river, and at its visual highspot the Thames, or part of it, runs across a grassy lawn with serene stone cottages lining it. More little bridges cross, and you could leap from bank to bank.

There is little more to tell. Paths lead on to Somerford Keynes, then an old church path follows the Thames to Ewen hamlet, crossing the stream by rickety footbridge. Just beyond Kemble, a last footpath sign points the way up the valley, and at most times of the year, the Thames water will cease to flow quite abruptly at a spring marked by a windpump. But this is not the source. Continue up the valley and trace the line of a dry stream, even find the faint suggestion of a simple footbridge that must once have been needed. Then over Foss Way a distant grove of trees attracts you up the same gentle valley, and there you will find the ring of pebbles that is the Thames spring. Only a simple inscribed stone beneath an ash tree, provided by the old Conservators of the Thames, tells you that your journey's end is here. A quiet spot in the foothills of the Cotswolds, in total contrast to the journey's beginning in London SW15. Why do we find such significance in a river's source? Is it because we sense the river itself as a life force, born in such a modest way, drawing life from its tributaries on the way to achieving great things? Whatever instinct brought us here, having followed all this way we seem to have reached a special relationship with Old Father Thames, to know it as others do not.

However you set out to explore the river, I recommend you to treat the Thames Walk as your essential guide. As the river is always conspicuously present and the aim of the walk is to keep near it, this might seem unnecessary advice. But the towpath does not always start off in the obvious fashion you would expect. In Cookham, for example, I have known people quite baffled as to how to follow the river in either direction. Or take the diversion problem: you could stand on the bridge at Goring, aware that there are no less than three missing ferries before the next upstream crossing. You might toss a coin on whether a north bank or south bank route would provide the best way round. The Thames Walk has tried out all the alternatives and opted for the best one.

One day perhaps it will be able to offer an even better route, but try it now. You could take twelve days or twelve years over it—rivers are not for rushing along. There is too much to see, too many tempting banks to recline upon. Fred Thacker, the historian of the Thames who tramped the river in the early 1900s, found a quotation that summed it up to perfection: 'Rivers were made for wise men to contemplate and fools to pass by without consideration.'

The Thames Walk

Progressive Mileage	Miles Between	Places on route	Bus services to	Rail Service	Cafes	Accommodation	Inns providing snacks etc	Shops	Camping
-	-	Putney		●	●		●	●	
8½	8½	Richmond	Many London Transport and London Country services	●	●	●	●	●	
12½	4	Kingston		●	●	●	●	●	
27½	15	Staines		●	●		●	●	Laleham Park
35	7½	Windsor		●	●	●	●	●	
42	7	Maidenhead	Cookham, Marlow	●	●		●	●	Hurley Farm
58	16	Henley	Shiplake, Reading	●	●	●	●	●	
66½	8½	Reading	Wallingford, Oxford, Henley	●	●	●	●	●	
73	6½	Pangbourne, Whitchurch	Reading, Oxford	●			●	●	
77	4	Goring, Streatley	As above	●		●	●	●	
83	6	Wallingford	As above		●	●	●	●	Wallingford, Municipal site
97½	14½	Abingdon	Wallingford, Didcot, Oxford		●	●	●	●	Sandford, Temple Farm
106½	9	Oxford	Reading, Swinford Bridge, Farringdon, Buckland etc.	●	●	●	●	●	Bablock Hythe
120½	14	Newbridge	—			●	●		
127½	7	Bampton (Rushy Weir)	Lechlade, Swindon			●	●	●	Radcot Bridge
136	8½	Lechlade	Swindon		●	●	●	●	Lechlade, by river
142½	6½	Castle Eaton	—			●	●		
146	3½	Cricklade	Swindon			●	●	●	Castle Eaton, Red Lion
151	5	Ashton Keynes				●	●		
157½	6½	Thames Head, Kemble		●			●	●	

There are youth hostels at Inglesham, Oxford, Streatley, Henley, Windsor, and the two London hostels at Earls Court and Holland House are 2 miles away from the river.

Outside the London area, bus services are operated from Reading by Alder Valley, 3 Thorn Walk, Reading, Berks. From Oxford by Oxford-South Midland, 395 Cowley Road, Oxford. From Swindon by Bristol Omnibus, Berkeley House, Lawrence Hill, Bristol

Glyndwr's Way

Keith Thorrington

Between the much-visited splendours of North Wales and Snowdonia and the no less popular Brecon Beacons and Black Mountains to the south, lies a quiet upland area, now in Powys but originally comprising the old Welsh counties of Radnorshire and part of Montgomeryshire. Essentially a rural, working region, it is characterised by short, steep valleys and hills where sheep rearing is the main activity. There are few dramatic changes in the scenery, although the rivers are an attractive feature and the huge Clywedog Dam with its spectacular reservoir behind it, present an astonishing variation in the general scene. In the valleys are villages and settlements—working communities where life has not greatly changed over the years, and in the few market towns old traditions still carry on. Here, you can truthfully say, is a region off the 'tourist beat' where visitors are few—but are still made very welcome.

Through this remote, rural countryside, I set out in the spring of 1979 to explore Glyndwr's Way, a long-distance footpath of 115 miles created by the Planning Department of Powys County Council. This then, is one rambler's view of a route, tried just two years after it had been opened throughout, with signposting and waymarking to praiseworthy standards, but still with some of the flaws to be expected in such a new venture. Inevitably in a largely agricultural region, the route becomes obscure at times as it threads its way between farms and villages. Some might be taken aback at the amount of road walking too, where there is as yet no footpath alternative. The roads, however, are so quiet, with the average volume of traffic perhaps a farmer's Land-Rover every hour or so, that this presents little real hardship.

The route has some memorably beautiful sections, and although not offering the spectacular, has plenty of variety throughout. Accommodation is relatively easy to find, and the farmhouses in particular provide wonderful value and can be especially recommended.

Normal walkers' equipment is all that is required, although it should be remembered that, due to the particular terrain, weather changes can be very frequent. Make sure, therefore, that your wet-weather gear is efficient. Some sections of the Way cross moorland where tracks are indistinct, so a compass of the Silva type is essential for peace of mind. Although the route is not a strenuous one, the extremely steep 'up and down' of the short Radnorshire hills can be tiring and weight in your rucksack should be kept to a minimum. If the route can be said to have an idiosyncrasy, it is its penchant for taking to the hills whenever possible. The subsequent short, steep climbs and descents can reveal some splendid views, but in heavy mist or rain when visibility is poor, there is little point in sticking rigidly to the route when there are alternatives along the valleys.

The walk will take you through many farmyards, but never once did I encounter any hostility to the walker. As one rugged hill farmer put it—'leave things as you find them and you're welcome'. The same

In this sheep-raising region, the secure shutting of gates is vital (*Geographical Magazine*)

Parliament House, Machynlleth

Glyndwr's Way descending from Plynlimon foothills

Kerry Hill ewe and lamb

Old lead mine and Llyn Clywedog Dam

philosophy does not extend unfortunately to the farm dogs who will inevitably rush the stranger, making a great to-do. They are not vicious, however, in my experience and as the same farmer remarked— 'their bark's worse than their bite!'

In this sheep-raising region, the secure shutting of gates is vital, as sheep, and especially lambs, are adept at wriggling through the smallest opening. Radnorshire gates, incidentally, tend to be secured by primitive devices, usually several feet of string or twistings of thick wire. It is generally quicker to climb over, if the gate is stout enough. Where it is not, beware that the whole contrivance does not collapse in a heap on the ground after you have untied it!

Students of Welsh history will recognise the significance of the name Glyndwr, after whom the Way is named. Owain Glyndwr, was a notable Welsh warrior, some say a Welsh hero, of the fifteenth century who, in his struggles against the English, came close to his goal of setting up a separate Welsh state. In the end he failed, and even his final burial place is disputed. His raids left the countryside in ruins with castles, towns and manors devastated, but he is claimed to have 'rekindled the flame of nationality', something which Wales has never forgotten. Glyndwr's Way passes close to the sites of incidents in the uprising, and through the market town of Machynlleth where Owain Glyndwr set up a Welsh Parliament.

Although the towns of Knighton and Welshpool are given as starting or finishing points for Glyndwr's Way, both places connect with the Countryside Commission's Offa's Dyke long-distance path. By using the section of Offa's Dyke path between Knighton and Welshpool, Glyndwr's Way becomes effectively a circular walk and can thus be joined anywhere along the route. Both towns are situated on the railway, with fairly frequent services to Shrewsbury.

Knighton to Machynlleth

Knighton is an attractive old town, offering plenty of accommodation. The route starts by the lofty clock tower and climbs up the Narrows, a picturesque street lined with small shops and somewhat reminiscent of the Shambles in York, to take a steep minor road around the flank of Garth Hill. All this area near Knighton suffered from Glyndwr's raids, and he effectively destroyed a castle once sited to the west of the town.

Although not on our route and some miles south-west of Knighton, anyone interested in Glyndwr's exploits should certainly visit Pilleth, now a farming settlement, which is the site of one of his greatest victories. The Battle of Pilleth is said to have taken place in 1402 between Glyndwr's followers and the army of Sir Edmund Mortimer, who held land in the county and along the Welsh border. Accounts vary, with estimates of the dead ranging from 200 to 8,000. It seems certain, however, that it represented a great victory for Glyndwr and was decisive in establishing his identity as a Welsh leader.

Looking back as the route climbs towards open moorland, there are fine views of Knighton spread out below. The road, running at an average height of over 1200ft, reaches Fountain Head and then follows tracks towards the village of Llancoch. This is an area of high moorland with wide-ranging views in all directions, but care has to be taken in route-finding as tracks are indistinct and waymarking scarce.

A typical Radnorshire scene from Glyndwr's Way near Llangunllo (*Keith Thorrington*)

From Llancoch the route turns west to reach more high moorland at heights of over 1500ft. Again, the tracks tend to get lost in the heather. On this section, one of the most demanding on the Way, it is best to set a compass course and check your position as often as possible. The route turns northwards over Black Mountain, an undefined section on the Ordnance Survey map, and makes for our destination of Felindre. Despite the route-finding problems, the views on a clear day from this high moorland are more than adequate compensation. This is a part of Glyndwr's Way to be lingered over, for it is one of the finest.

Nearing Felindre, the route, well waymarked now, turns briefly eastwards past Brandy House Farm and then the village, set prettily on the river Teme, is there below you. Felindre is a small working community where you should find accommodation at one of the farms. There is said to be a working forge here and the village is especially proud of its unusual asset of an international tug-of-war team. Many of the team's trophies are displayed at the Wharf Inn.

Beyond the village, the Way heads west along a ridge track. There are good views down to the Teme valley and this is an area notable for Bronze-Age tumuli. The track reaches a crossroads of paths and bridleways and then, possibly because of route-finding difficulties, turns north-west instead of south as might be expected, to join a road for 3 miles into the village of Llanbadarn Fynydd. Walkers with time in hand could avoid a rather lengthy road walk, though one with fine views, by exploring the possibilities of the many alternative bridleways shown leading southwards on the OS map. A logical route could be the bridleway past Bryngydfa and then the track marked Fron Top leading directly into Llanbadarn Fynydd.

The village straggles along the busy A483 road, but is attractively situated on the river Ithon with a useful inn and shop. Our route crosses the river and heads due west for a mile or so before turning south towards the hill of Moel-dod. An interesting diversion can be taken to visit the derelict settlement of New Well, just to the west of Moel-dod. In a deep valley by the Crychell Brook, there was a flourishing community here up to the end of the nineteenth century. Then, in common with the rest of this part of Wales, the population declined and the settlement was abandoned. There is said to have been a school, shop and post office here. The ruined buildings can be seen still, and the overgrown track which led to them can be traced for some distance.

The official route, joined again $\frac{1}{2}$ mile from the ruins, descends south-eastwards and on a clear day the remains of an old fortification called Castelltinboeth can be seen on the far side of the Ithon valley. The fort is said to have been named after Maud de Breos, wife of Roger, a member of the Mortimer family prominent in the area in the fourteenth century. Earlier it is thought to have been the residence of Cadwallon ap Madoc, a likely founder of Abbey Cwmhir, our destination for the day's walk.

The Way soon joins a road beside Bachell Brook which leads directly to Abbey Cwmhir. The village is named after the great Cistercian abbey founded in 1143, which dominated this area until it was destroyed by Owain Glyndwr in 1401. The ruins can still be seen nearby, although much of the stone has been taken for other buildings. The abbey was never fully completed, but it was intended to be one of the largest in Britain. The imposing manor house on the right as you enter the village is The Hall, built in mock-Elizabethan style with stone taken from the abbey ruins in the early 1800s. There is accommodation, a shop and inn, the Happy Union, in the village. The inn sign is most unusual—a man with a leek in his hat riding a goat and holding up an ale jug and plate!

Glyndwr's Way leaves the village by a forest track down to Clywedog Brook, where the ford may be difficult in times of flood. At the tumulus of Castell-y-garn, an ancient trackway known as the Monk's Way is joined, thought to have been the route between Abbey Cwmhir and Strata Florida in Dyfed. It leads on into the isolated village of Bwlch-y-Sarnau. Now follows an energetic and somewhat eccentric route, alternating between stretches of moor and forest, where the Way takes to the 'short and steep hills' with a vengeance! After skirting the side of Baily Hill, stretches of forest follow until the route reaches high moorland at Blaentrinant. The views here from a height of around 1300ft are exceptional on a clear day and can extend to the Plynlimons and as far as Cader Idris.

After Blaentrinant, the route becomes devious and a close watch must be kept on the map or waymarks where they are in evidence.

Signpost on Glyndŵr's Way

The walk switches direction disconcertingly as it threads its way towards the next highlight above the settlement of Newchapel. Here a glorious view stretches away towards the Severn valley some 500ft below. Now the route descends towards Llanidloes, a market town on the Severn recommended as a stopping place.

Llanidloes, where Welsh is spoken as an everyday language, has as its focal point the Old Market Hall, a unique timber-framed building standing in the middle of the town at the crossroads. The upper floor now houses the museum and underneath is an open cobble-stoned market place where a market, said to date from 1280, is still held every Saturday. Thirsty walkers can note that the public houses stay open all day on market days, a custom common in Wales. The town is a bright, busy place, where the occasional tourist tends to stand out as he strolls amongst the regulars. The traffic has a very rural air with numbers of battered Land-Rovers, bales of hay in the back, forming a good part of it. In the shops, the switch to English for the benefit of the visitor is off-putting at first, but it is done in a friendly way.

From the town, the route crosses the river Severn over Long Bridge and follows roads to the village of Fan. A hundred years ago, this area was the scene of a mining boom in lead and zinc, and the Fan mine was one of the largest producers of lead in the country. The village, though still inhabited, now has a desolate air with heaps of spoil stretching for acres nearby. The old mine buildings are slowly crumbling away. Although environmentalists may point to this as an example of shocking neglect, it must be borne in mind that a hundred years or more has to elapse before vegetation will start to grow again on land used for lead-mining. It remains at the moment an interesting industrial relic and, no doubt, all this area will be cleared in the future and reclaimed. Nearby is Fan Pool, originally a reservoir for the mine but now a nature reserve with many waterfowl. The path climbs again, then takes the approach track to a farm. From here, in a few more yards, we are high above the huge dam of Clywedog, towering over 200ft and a re-markably dramatic sight as it first comes into view. The Way descends sharply in a series of zigzags to the Clywedog valley. In times of excep-tional rainfall the reservoir has a controlled means of overflow, and the Dam appears even more spectacular when seen in these circumstances.

Below, almost directly under the dam, are the remains of the old lead barytes mine of Brytail. The buildings here are slowly being restored by the Department of the Environment as an industrial monument. The remains of the old mine and the mighty, modern dam a few feet away, make an interesting industrial contrast. The Afon Clywedog, infant or turbulent according to the overflow, is crossed by a high footbridge and Glyndwr's Way now climbs towards the reser-voir. A viewpoint near the road gives some impressive details—completed in December 1967, it is $6\frac{1}{2}$ miles long and holds no less than 11,000 million gallons. It was designed to control the flow of the river Severn and to ensure water supplies to the Severn valley even in times of drought. Man-made though it may be, Clywedog with its irregular shoreline has the appearance of a natural lake, and it is difficult to deny its beauty.

The Way now shares a nature trail which leads down near the lake. It then joins the lakeside road but although there is grass to walk on, a separate path would be preferable to separate the walker from the traffic and cars parked along the verge. At the end of the lake the road leads into Hafren Forest. The official route takes a short cut here, but I found it flooded and strewn with fallen trees. It may well be clear now. Hafren Forest is a conifer plantation covering some 17 square miles, and presents a gloomy spectacle on a dull day. Just after the road leaves it to cross the stream of Afon Llwyd, there are reminders of the warrior Glyndwr again. Three miles to the west, by the valley of Afon Hyddgen, Glyndwr and his men gained a victory against heavy odds. The result of the battle, fought in 1401, rallied more men to his cause.

The Way continues along the road—rather a long road section this—to a junction, and walkers ending this stage in Staylittle should turn right here to find the village just a few yards further on. Its unusual name is said to have derived from a speedy blacksmith who reshod horses so quickly that travellers only had to 'stay a little'.

Continuing to Dylife, the Way takes a track past a cemetery known as the Quaker Garden. Quakers are said to have predominated in the area during the late seventeenth and early eighteenth centuries. The track ascends past Rhiw-defeitty-fawr Farm towards high moorland, now following the course of a Roman road used until the end of the stage-coach era as the route between Llanidloes and Machynlleth. Below lies our destination of Dylife which, like Fan, is on the site of a long-disused metal mine. The only inhabited buildings remaining are the rectory and the Star Inn, which looks out over extensive heaps of spoil and waste land. In its heyday, Dylife had a population of over 1,000 but in 1920 the deposits of copper, lead and zinc were exhausted and the mine abandoned.

The Roman road is rejoined above Dylife for a steady climb to nearly 1700ft. The Glyndwr's Way sign directs us to a track on the left and we begin to ascend the Plynlimon foothills. The track skirts the deep and spectacular Foel Fadian gorge, and on its far side Glaslyn Lake or 'Blue Lake' can be seen clearly in the distance. This is wild, mountainous terrain with wide-ranging views. The route descends slowly down a deep valley towards the farm of Nant y Fyda, crosses the Afon Dulas and takes tracks across the hills to the village of Forge. Shortly afterwards, Machynlleth is entered by the main Aberystwyth road.

Glyndwr's Way descending from the Plynlimon foothills (*Keith Thorrington*)

Machynlleth is on the railway with services to the coast or Shrews-bury and with buses to many parts. Here, briefly, we enter a more tourist-conscious area. The beautiful Dovey valley is nearby and the heady attractions of Aberystwyth a few miles away. The town has some fine architecture and the most impressive building is the Owain Glyndwr Institute of black and white timbers, which dates from the eighteenth century. Now used by the Mid-Wales Tourist Board, it is a reminder of the part Glyndwr played here. Just adjacent to the Institute, the Parliament House of sixteenth-century origin is said to mark the site where he was proclaimed Prince of Wales in 1404. There followed the establishment of a Welsh Parliament and plans for two universities. The following year Glyndwr was involved in the Tripartite Indenture, a plan to overthrow King Henry IV and divide England and Wales between Glyndwr and his two conspiritors, Edmund Mortimer and the Earl of Northumberland. Glyndwr was to rule Wales and a large part of England. In the end, however, the plot failed. Despite help from Charles VI of France with whom Glyndwr formed an alliance, a decisive victory over the English was not won and the French returned home.

Machynlleth to Welshpool

The section of Glyndwr's Way starting from Machynlleth is unfortunately the least inviting of the whole route, and involves a 4 mile trudge along a main road before a track is reached leading to quieter parts. I am sure there is a good reason why this particular section was decided upon by the planners of the Way, but the fact remains that, for the walker, the 4 miles along the busy A489 are most unpleasant and potentially dangerous. Some route problems are inevitable at this early stage, but it is to be hoped that Powys CC have this section under urgent review and will publish an alternative.

A mile beyond the village of Penegoes, the route turns off the main road for a track to Corregyfudde Farm. I found no signposts or waymarking on this section, but they appear again after passing through Abercegir. This is an attractively situated old village, once a centre for the woollen industry, entered by a footbridge over a stream close to an old mill, the last of many in the area and now abandoned.

From the village, the Way climbs steep meadows to a fine open stretch of hillside, with good views on a clear day towards Cader Idris and the Aran range. Some of the tracks here are indistinct and a course should be set towards Cemmaes Road, a village further along the A489 at the junction of the main road from Newtown and by the confluence of the rivers Dovey and Tywyn. A mile west of the village is the ancient residence of Mathafarn, another haunt of Owain Glyndwr, who is said to have made a secret tunnel from here to the Parliament House at Machynlleth. Part of the old house dates back to the 1600s.

Out of Cemmaes Road, the route follows the A489 again for a short stretch, crosses the Tywyn and then takes a track over the hills towards the settlement of Commins Gwalia. This is open hill country with sweeping views of the Dyfi valley and towards the river Tywyn. The Way now descends to the Newtown road leading to Llanbrynmair, a sizeable village recommended as the next stopping place. From the south-east end of the village, a farmyard, very muddy in wet conditions, is negotiated and a high upland region gained by fields and a series of gates. The track is fairly well defined, though without signs or waymarks.

A few miles further on, 1000ft up among the lonely hills, my Glyndwr's Way floundered and came to a halt. According to the route and the map, the track should continue through a conifer plantation to reach a minor road a mile further on. Entry to the conifers and an indistinct opening beyond was effectively barred, however, by a stout wire fence with a barbed wire top. Let us hope this is another section under review. I followed the line of the plantation north-eastwards over the moor, crossed a boggy bit where two bootfuls of water were acquired, then followed a very ancient-looking sunken trackway marked in black on the OS map, to reach the road.

This is a very wild part of the Way and, although a road is now followed, it is a mere narrow ribbon amongst the rolling hill country. The dashing waters of the Afon Gam, running beside the road for miles, make a musical sound in the wilderness. Traffic, apart from a Land-Rover or two, is non-existent. After a few miles, the Way leaves the road near Dolwen Farm and climbs high up above the road and river to follow tracks to the village of Llangadfan. A well-known Welsh poet of the eighteenth century, William Jones, is buried in the churchyard here, and the village is notable for the unusually named Cann Office Hotel, said to be derived from the Welsh 'Cae'n y ffos' meaning fortified or ditched enclosure. An earthwork by the hotel is the remains of a Norman-style castle thought to date from the thirteenth century.

North-east of the village, the route turns towards the large Dyfnant Forest. I must confess now that, due to very wet weather conditions, a dislike of walking through forests and an ominous mention of crossing a 'maze of forestry tracks' in the route description, I did not follow the official course of the Way religiously for the next few miles. Instead I took the relatively traffic-free B4395 and than a metalled track leading through the forest by the side of the Afon Vyrnwy. This alternative is straightforward and very pleasant walking. Although still through a forestry area, it is not enveloped by trees and there are open views on several sections. Dyfnant Forest is nearly all conifer, and for those interested I understand there are large specimens of cypress, red cedar, lodgepole pine, Scots pine, Douglas fir, Norway spruce and grande fir to be seen.

The track reaches a hairpin bend on the B4393 road at a height of some 900ft and joining it, descends towards Llanwddyn and Lake Vyrnwy. The lake is one of Britain's oldest reservoirs, opened in 1888. Nearly 5 miles long and averaging $\frac{1}{2}$ mile across, it is not nearly as scenically attractive as Clywedog. An interesting relic on the hill above, near Lake Vyrnwy Hotel, is a memorial to the workmen killed during its eight-year construction.

Strong walkers may attempt the 26 miles on from Llanwddyn to Welshpool in one day. Far better, I feel, to break the journey at Meifod, leaving plenty of time the following day to visit Powys Castle. Leaving the Victorian atmosphere of Lake Vyrnwy, the Way retraces the walk of yesterday up to the hairpin bend, then by tracks and minor roads into the village of Llwydiarth. From here a track by the Afon Vyrnwy is followed for a stretch, then a rather uncertain route over fields towards the next village of Dolanog. Meifod, reached by further field paths and tracks through very rural, isolated countryside, is a sizeable village on the Afon Vyrnwy.

As the end of the Way approaches, perhaps a few words should be added about those inoffensive woolly creatures who have watched our progress through mid-Wales. It is not surprising to learn that the Powys sheep account for 5% of the entire Common Market flocks, and anyone interested can find fascinating details about their management, shearing, sales and different breeds in a remarkably informative leaflet produced by Powys CC, price 12p including postage. For the un-informed walker, the reaction of sheep to his progress through their fields can be most amusing. Some will look on indifferently and quickly resume their busy munching. Others will run off in panic and then return to survey the intruder indignantly. Still others may regard you as their natural leader and two or three dozen, all baaing raucously, will follow docilely as far as they can. It is quite likely that you will be able to free lambs or even sheep stuck halfway through fences or gates during the walk, this emphasising their urge to stray at every opportunity.

The last few miles from Meifod are mostly along quiet lanes and bring us quickly to Welshpool, a busy market town in the Severn valley and not far from the Shropshire border. Powys Castle and its

End of the walk—Powys Castle, Welshpool (*Keith Thorrington*)

extensive grounds dominate the town and should certainly be visited. The castle is said to have been started in the eleventh century and in more recent times was refurbished during the reign of Elizabeth I. The well-known landscape gardener Capability Brown designed the grounds and gardens in the early nineteenth century, and they remain today a fitting tribute to his skill, with terraces on different levels and carefully tended plants and trees setting off the looming castle above. The castle and grounds are open from May to September excepting Mondays and there is easy pedestrian access from the middle of the town.

For walkers wishing to continue on to Knighton and make a round trip of Glyndwr's Way, Offa's Dyke path can be picked up at the village of Hope, two miles east of Welshpool. But many will end their Glyndwr's Way expedition at Welshpool, and there will be few who have not enjoyed it and the insight gained into a remoter part of Britain. If it is not perfect at its present stage of development, this in no way detracts from the enterprise of Powys County Council in devising it. Glyndwr's Way should serve as a model to other county councils and the more people who walk it, the better it will become.

Glyndwr's Way

Progressive Mileage	Miles Between	Places on route	Bus service to	Rail Service	Cafes	Accommodation	Inns providing snacks etc	Shops	Camping
-	-	Knighton	Market Drayton, Newcastle-under-Lyme	●	●	●	●	●	Heartsease Farm
14	14	Felindre	—			●	●	●	Brandy House Farm, Criggen Farm, Upper Home Farm
21½	7½	Llanbadarn Fynydd	—			●	●	●	Brook Cottage, New Inn
29	7½	Abbey Cwmhir	—			●	●	●	Happy Union Inn
44	15	Llanidloes	Newtown, Rhayader, Shrewsbury, Welshpool	●	●	●	●		
55	11	Staylittle	—			●	●	●	Rhiwdyfeity Farm
68	13	Machynlleth	Aberystwyth, Newtown	●	●	●	●	●	Llwyn Farm Penegoes
78	10	Cemmaes Road	Machynlleth, Newtown			●	●		
83	5	Llanbrynmair	Machynlleth, Newtown			●	●	●	Dolgadfan Farm, Bronder-wgoed Farm
93	10	Llangadfan	—			●	●		
100	7	Lake Vynwy	—			●	●	●	Fron Heulog, Llanwddyn
110	10	Dolanog	—			●	●		
116	6	Meifod	—			●	●	●	Tanyllyn
124	8	Welshpool	Oswestry, Llanidloes, Newtown, Shrewsbury	●	●	●	●	●	Maesygro Farm Leighton, Gortheur Farm Leighton

There is a youth hostel at Knighton, but others at Nant-y-Dernol, Corris and Dinas Mawddwy are only within hitching distance. A hostel on the coast at Borth is a few miles from Machynlleth on the Aberystwyth line

Early closing: Thursday afternoon in Llanidloes, Machynlleth and Welshpool

Some bus services are very infrequent. A useful train and bus timetable can be obtained from the Development Board for Rural Wales, Ladywell House, Newtown, Powys SY16 1JB, Price 35p plus 15p postage

Appendix

Dales Way
Maps
OS 1:50 000 sheets 97, 98 and 104
OS 1:25 000 Outdoor Leisure maps: Malham and Upper Wharfedale (Grassington to Beckermonds); Three Peaks (Beckermonds to Lower Dentdale); English Lakes SE (Grayrigg Foot to Bowness)
Also very useful are the 1:25 000 Footpath maps by Arthur Gemmell; Bolton Abbey District; Sedbergh District; Sedbergh Howgills. From Stile Maps, Mercury House, Otley, West Yorkshire, 25p each plus postage.

Guides
The Dales Way by Colin Speakman, a comprehensive paperback guide to the route. Dalesman Publishing Company, Clapham, Lancaster, £1.20 plus postage. *Dales Way Handbook* by RA West Riding Area. Revised annually, it includes latest information on rights of way, accommodation and public transport. From Ramblers' Association National Office, 1/5 Wandsworth Road, London SW8 2LJ, 20p plus postage.

Other path guides
Parklink walks in Upper Wharfedale by Arthur Gemmell, Stile Publications as above, 45p plus postage.

Three Forests Way
Maps
OS 1:50 000 sheet 167 plus very short sections on sheets 166 and 177.

Guide
The Three Forests Way by Fred Matthews and Harry Bitten. A 44-page guide with section by section sketch maps and detailed route description, from the author, Fred Matthews, Glen View, London Road, Abridge, Essex, 45p plus postage. Also a cloth badge on completion of the route, 50p plus postage.

Other path guides
Short Walks in West Essex. Twenty short round walks from car parks, 75p plus postage. *Short Walks in London's Epping Forest*, twenty 3-mile round

interlocked walks, 60p plus postage. Both from Fred Matthews as above. *Walks on the Herts and West Essex Border* from local bookshops in the Bishops Stortford area, price 50p.

Viking Way
Maps
OS 1:50 000 sheets 112, 113, 121, 130, 141 (last 4 miles only).

Guides
Complete route guide published by Lincoln RA Group. Details from Major Brett Collier, 'Lukenya', Hillfoot, North Carlton, Lincoln.

Viking Way Information Leaflets
Humber Bridge to Bigby—free leaflet (s.a.e.) from The Director of Technical Services, Humberside County Council, Eastgate, Beverley.
Bigby to Woolsthorpe—Six section leaflets from the Head of Secretarial & Legal Services, Lincolnshire County Council, County Offices, Newland, Lincoln, 5p each leaflet plus postage. Also outline route map (6 miles to 1 inch).
Woolsthorpe to Oakham—leaflet from County Planning Officer, Leicestershire County Council, County Hall, Glenfield, Leicester, 5p plus s.a.e. (These information leaflets are not route guides and OS maps are necessary). Bardney to Lincoln—route guide for the local Ramblers' Association alternative route, from RA Lincoln Group, address as above. 8p plus s.a.e.

Accommodation List from RA Lincoln Group as above, 20p plus s.a.e. Also a cloth badge on completion of route, 50p plus s.a.e.

Oxfordshire Way
Maps
OS 1:50 000 sheets 163, 164, 165 (fraction only) and 175.
CPRE strip maps specially drawn at 1:25 000 on three large sheets, from the Branch Secretary, CPRE Oxfordshire, Sandford Mount, Charlbury, Oxford, 40p each or £1 the set post free.

Guide
The Oxfordshire Way by Alison Kemp gives full directions on the route, together with accommodation, refreshment facilities, transport services and interesting features along the way. Also a distance table and a diagram showing the sheet boundaries of all maps covering the route. From CPRE Oxfordshire as above, 60p post free.

Two Moors Way

Maps

OS 1:50 000 sheets 180, 181, 191 and 202.

OS 1in Tourist Exmoor and Dartmoor sheets between them cover the whole route.

Guide

Two Moors Way, 34 pages of maps at 1:18 000 with notes on places of interest and route directions where necessary to help both north- and south-bound wayfarers. Includes accommodation list. From J. R. Turner, Coppins, The Poplars, Pinhoe, Exeter, Devon EX4 9HH. 65p plus postage.

Cumbria Way

Maps

OS 1:50 000 sheets 85, 90 and 97.

OS 1in Tourist map of the Lake District covers the route from Broughton Beck to Caldbeck.

OS 1:25 000 Outdoor Leisure maps: English Lakes SW (Beacon Tarn to Colwith Force, and Elterwater to Langstrath); English Lakes SE (Low Yewdale to Chapel Stile); English Lakes NW (Stake Pass to Skiddaw House).

Guide

Cumbria Way by John Trevelyan, Dalesman 50p, or from RA Lake District Area, 62 Loop Road, North Whitehaven, Cumbria, 50p plus postage.

Other path guides

Park your car and take a walk II by RA Furness Group. From RA Lake District Area as above, 60p plus postage.

Walking in Central Lakeland by Brian and Jay Greenwood (Dalesman) and *Walking in Northern Lakeland* by Peter Lewis and Brian Porter (Dalesman). Both from RA Lake District Area as above, 70p and 75p respectively, plus postage.

North Bucks Way

Maps

OS 1-50 000 North Bucks Way sheets 152 and 165; Grafton & Knightley Ways sheet 152.

Guides

The North Buckinghamshire Way. Strip maps at 1in to the mile, route direc-
‑ions and brief notes on the villages, with a section on transport, accom-

modation and refreshment facilities. From Ramblers' Association Southern Area, 1/5 Wandsworth Road, London SW8 2LJ, 15p plus postage. *The Knightley Way* and *The Grafton Way*, two leaflets with route directions from Northampton County Leisure and Amenities Dept, Northampton House, Northampton NN1 2JP, 5p each with s.a.e.

Other path guides
On foot in the Vale of Aylesbury by Peter and Diana Gulland, eighteen short circular walks. From RA Southern Area as above, 90p plus postage.

Coast to Coast Walk

Maps
OS 1-50 000 sheets 89, 90, 91, 92, 93, 94, 98 and 99
OS 1in Tourist maps Lake District (Ennerdale to Shap) and North York Moors (Ingleby Cross to Robin Hood's Bay).

Guide
A Coast to Coast Walk by A. Wainwright. A small hardback book in annotated strip-map style, with every word hand-drawn as well as the maps and illustrations, full route directions with much detail in his very personal style. Westmorland Gazette, Stricklandgate, Kendal. £2.25 plus postage.

Cotswold Way

Maps
OS 1:50 000 sheets 150 (2 miles only), 151, 162, 163 and 172.
The Way will eventually be covered by six specially drawn three-colour maps at 1:25 000, with the Way boldly marked. Two published so far, others in preparation. Details from RA Gloucestershire Area, Bill Bingley, Jasmine Cottage, Knightsbridge, Cheltenham, Gloucestershire.

Guides
The Cotswold Way by Mark Richards. Beautifully drawn strip maps at 1:25 000 with illustrations in Wainwright style, no text but some hints on finding the route included on maps. Second edition. From RA National Office or from RA Gloucestershire Area as above, 85p plus postage. New redrawn edition in preparation.
Cotswold Way Handbook. Updated every year or two. Lists eighty-five accommodation addresses with information on transport, camping, refreshments, walking schedules. From RA Gloucestershire Area as above, 20p plus postage.

Ebor Way

Maps
OS 1:50 000 sheets 100, 104, and 105.

Guide
The Ebor Way by J. K. E. Piggin, gives detailed route directions. From the author, 95 Bishopthorpe Road, York, YO2 1NX or from Dalesman, £1 plus postage. Leaflets listing accommodation, camp sites and other information including any changes in the route, from J. K. E. Piggin as above on receipt of s.a.e. Also badges and completion cards.

Other path guides
Walks north of York by Geoffrey White and Geoffrey Green. Dalesman, 75p plus postage. *Walks in the Vale of York* by RA York Group. From D. Nunns, 26 Fir Tree Close, York, 85p plus postage. *More Wetherby and Tadcaster Footpath Walks* from D. Rawson, 23 Foxhill, Wetherby, 60p plus postage. *Otley and District Footpath Map and Guide* from the Secretary, Hilton Grange School, Old Bramhope, Leeds LS16 9HO, 25p plus postage.

Thames Walk

Maps
OS 1:50 000 sheets 163, 164, 174 (fraction), 175, and 176.

Guide
to the towpath walk and the diversions currently necessary published by Ramblers' Association Southern Area. Details from RA Southern Area, address as above.

Glyndwr's Way

Maps
OS 1:50 000 sheets 125, 126, 135, 136, and 148.

Guide
Glyndwr's Way: a set of sixteen leaflets, each describing a 6 to 11 mile section, with maps and full description, from the Planning Department, Powys County Council, Llandrindod Wells, Powys, 80p plus postage. Also *Glyndwr's Way Accommodation List* from the same address 5p plus postage.